CW00832225

BERMUDA
DICK

When I first commenced my journey,
Many said he'll turn again,
But they have all been deceived,
In the way I still remain.

Many years have now elapsed,
Since I first began to pray;
I have been in many a conflict,
But I am here alive today.

(from 'The Pilgrims Song' *c.* 1858)
GRO D2598 1/28

BERMUDA DICK

The true story of Forest of Dean convicts …

Averil Kear

 **Lightmoor Press**

British Library Cataloguing-in-Publication Data. A catalogue
record for this book is available from the British Library
ISBN 1 899889 08 6

Lightmoor Press
47 – 49 High Street, Lydney, Gloucestershire GL15 5DD

Printed by The Alden Press, Oxford

CONTENTS

This book is dedicated
to my husband Alec for his long term patience and understanding;
and to Doug who went on the hardest journey of all.

Foreword

About ten years ago I started doing my husband's family history little knowing what I was to find out. Our name is Kear and the family has forever lived in the Forest of Dean area of Gloucestershire. When I got back to details of my husband's great-great grandfather, I discovered that he had left a will. This will left money to his son 'now residing in Bermuda'.

Thinking that we might be the owners of a beautiful property on that lovely island, my research began. On asking elderly members of the family if they knew anything about this we learnt that in fact the son Richard Kear had been sent to Bermuda for 'deer stealing'.

Research continued, Why Bermuda? and why deer stealing?

Details of assize records uncovered that Richard Kear had not been sent to Bermuda for 'deer stealing' but was in fact convicted of 'rape' along with six other men.

Over the last ten years my research has uncovered the whole story of conviction, imprisonment (in several prisons) and subsequent transportation to Bermuda to work on the building of the naval dockyard there. I also followed the story of two of the men who were sent elsewhere, one to Australia, after Bermuda, and the other from Dartmoor to Gibraltar.

Richard Kear did eventually return to the Forest of Dean, only to find that his wife, whom he had married shortly before his crime, had remarried. Richard found a new wife and they produced Grandfather Kear, hence the reason my husband and his family were still born in the Forest of Dean.

The period of this story is from 1825 when Richard Kear was born to the transportation in 1852, the events in Bermuda until 1861, subsequent imprisonment back in England for a couple of years and his life on return to the Forest of Dean.

All my research is backed up with complete document references from the Gloucestershire Record Office, Gloucester Local Studies Library, the Public Record Office at Kew, and many, many more. My husband and I also spent a very nostalgic holiday in Bermuda carrying out research and viewing the naval dockyard, which is today the Maritime Museum. We also found the tiny graveyard where two of the Forest of Dean men were buried after contracting Yellow Fever and we were able to erect a small gravestone in their memory.

I did not set out to write the history of penal servitude or to give full accounts of the prison system in Victorian times. Details of these have been covered with far more authority in many of the publications I have consulted.

I have tried to paint a picture of the prison conditions which were encountered by a particular group of men from the Forest of Dean in England, Bermuda and other parts of the world during the mid to late 19th century.

Averil Kear
2002

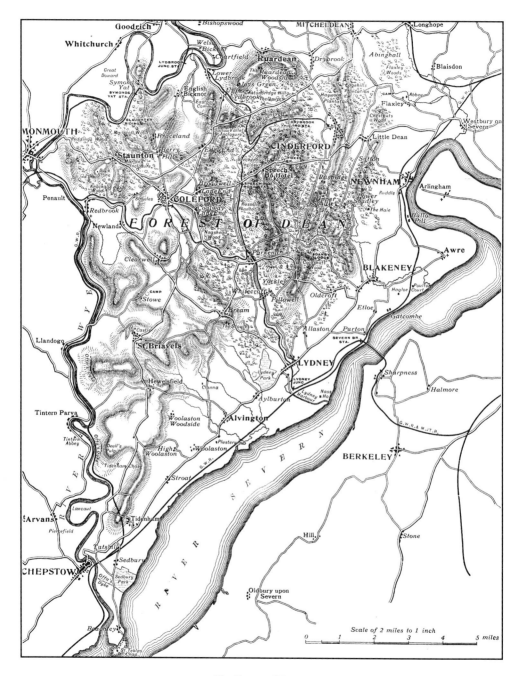

The Forest of Dean

Chapter One

FOREST DAYS

Richard Kear shifted his weight from one foot to the other to ease the pain from the iron shackles around his ankle, which bound him to the man in front. He had been branded a 'convict' and told that he was to be transported to a place called Bermuda. Richard did not know where this was only that there was work for convicts in Bermuda helping to build a naval dockyard. For the last few months Richard and three other men who had been convicted with him had been held at Portland prison in Dorset, and they were now waiting to board the *Edward* for a sea voyage which they had been told would last many days. Richard looked across at his friends but they did not return his gaze, their heads hung low and he could see that the spirit had gone out of their bodies. They felt the pull on the shackles as the line began to move up the gangplank. Richard shut his eyes and followed blindly wondering if he would ever see England or his home again.

Home was the Forest of Dean, which lies between the River Severn and the River Wye in that particular corner of Gloucestershire, which at the beginning of the 19th century was so inaccessible that it was virtually a country on its own. The name Forest of Dean was recorded from about 1080[1] probably named after a manor called Dean situated in the north of the Forest in the 11th century. At one time the whole Forest belonged to the Crown as a Royal hunting ground but gradually parishes and hamlets grew up within it and in the 1840s it was split into the two civil areas of East and West Dean, which in turn were split into ecclesiastical parishes. The Forest covers about 23,000 acres, which by the time young Richard Kear was growing up, contained some 11,000 acres of enclosed oak plantations used entirely for shipbuilding purposes. Although a great deal of the ancient woodland had been destroyed to make charcoal for the iron industry the great need for strong oaks for the navy ensured the survival of the Forest.

Many deer roamed the Forest in the 13th century, kept there for the royal huntsmen but the numbers were greatly reduced as the woods were cleared for the charcoal burners. The king still required deer for his hunting but by the 17th century they were becoming a nuisance in the new enclosures and an Act of 1668 limited the numbers to 800 only.[2] Richard Kear would not have seen many deer as the Crown Commissioners of Woods ordered their destruction in 1849. They felt that they were an 'inducement to poaching' which had demoralising effects on the Foresters. During the early part of the 19th century, Edward Machen the Crown Commissioners Deputy Surveyor of Woods employed keepers. Their job was to police and maintain the enclosures making sure that there was no illegal digging of turf and soil, no stealing of timber, no poaching, and no encroachment of land by the Forest inhabitants or their livestock onto the royal demesne.

Encroachers had moved into the Forest of Dean during the early 18th century and by 1803 there were nearly 3,000 men, women and children squatting there in about 600 cottages. These poor people were using an old belief that a man could choose any area of land within the Forest and build his house on it. If he managed to enclose this land and have a fire burning in his hearth in one day then the land was his by right. These occupants pastured their sheep, pigs and cattle on the commons in the Forest and kept small gardens and orchards. Richard Kear's grandfather William kept sheep and cattle, which after his death were sold to pay off his debts.

Both coal and iron ore are found in the Forest, the latter being worked by the Romans who used the Forest inhabitants to work for them. Certainly William the Conqueror laid a yearly charge on the city of Gloucester to provide him with iron, and in the time of Henry III laws were passed to cut the number of illegal forges in the Forest. A great deal of trouble was caused by the demands of miners who were cutting timber for shoring up their own mines and making charcoal to use in the iron furnaces. In 1612 a grant was made to the Earl of Pembroke stating that he had the sole right to dig for mine ore, cinders, stone and sea-coal (as it was then commonly called), and forbidding anyone else to take or carry out any of the Forest timber, ore, or cinders without his consent, save such timber as might be required for His Majesty's shipping.[3] The miners responded to this by rioting and they still continued to supply their iron ore to works outside the Forest.

The Crown from early days had always valued the skill of the Forest of Dean miners in excavating and burrowing, and the men were often used in armies both in Great Britain and overseas. After the Scottish wars in the 14th century the Crown rewarded the miners for their expertise by the granting of certain privileges.[4] Among these privileges the miners were allowed to take wood to shore up their work and to have access for carrying goods to public highways. In 1673 Richard Morse finally wrote down a list of these codes and practices, which, with the help of finance by the miners was eventually published in a booklet. The booklet was used in a long drawn out court case between the Teringham family and a Mr. Dennis, and was referred to as the book used against Dennis. This was eventually shortened to 'The Book of Dennis'.[5] These ancient Forest laws apply to the present day and initially covered the wider bounds of the Forest but by the mid 19th century only the smaller area of the Hundred of St. Briavels was allowed these special rights.

Coal mines and levels were worked during the 17th and 18th centuries under the government of the Mine Law Court, which met initially at St. Briavels Castle. The Constable of the Castle and his clerk, the Gaveller and miners who formed the jury, settled disputes between miners here. In 1680 this Court met at the Speech House, which then became its permanent venue. The Speech House was built about 1670 as one of six keeper's lodges and was originally called King's Lodge. Shortly before 1841 it was leased as an inn but remained as the meeting place of the court, by then called the verderers' court. This court still has the authority to meet today if required. The office of Gaveller, or keeper of the 'gale,' had been created by the Crown in 1464[6] to regulate the mining in the Forest of Dean and together with his deputies he alone was responsible for granting new claims to the free miners. The qualification to become a Freeminer is that a man should have been born within the Hundred of St. Briavels. He should have worked a year and a day at a mine within that Hundred, and some miners insist that he should be the son of a free father. It was the ambition of every coal miner to become a Freeminer thus allowing them the opportunity to dig for coal where they liked whether the land was leased to private individuals or not. Although there were some restrictions over the centuries, basically a man could choose his plot of ground and ask the deputy Gaveller to go to the place to grant him full possession. Freeminers considered that their special rights entitled them to claim timber for use in their pits, which led to many disputes between the Crown and the miners.

During the first half of the 19th century entrepreneurs realised the potential of the mineral wealth in the Forest of Dean and before too long were moving in. They brought wealth with them, which enabled them to buy up many mines making the free miners their employees. Other labourers from outside the Forest began to move in as the need for labour grew and the deputy Gaveller remonstrated with outside mine owners for employing other than Forest of Dean free miners. Large new collieries and iron works appeared in the Forest and tramroads, and later railways, were developed to cope with the increased production. The free miners became aware that labourers outside the Forest of Dean could earn much more than their 2/- to 8/- per week and many of them became increasingly unsettled with the battle for jobs between outsiders and Foresters.

When young Richard Kear was just three years old a great national depression hit the Forest causing high unemployment and great hardship. Foresters were forced to use their ancient rights by taking wood for their fires and using any part of the Forest to keep their animals on. The

Forest of Dean iron miners circa 1858.   H. G. Nicholls *Forest of Dean*

Commissioners of Woods were quite indifferent to the hardship caused by the slump and in 1829 reported that the rights of the free miners should be abolished and the Crown should solely administer the Forest using the minerals under the ground as it wished. The Commissioners also felt that a stop should be put to encroachments, which had nearly trebled in the last 40 years. The Foresters had taken enough and in 1831 Warren James called a band of men together and went out to break down the barriers erected by the Commissioners over the years to keep Foresters out. The riots continued for several months with many dissatisfied Foresters both men and women joining in. Police and troops were called in and eventually Warren James was arrested and subsequently transported to Australia. In 1832 the granting of gales to free miners was temporarily halted whilst the commissioners devised new regulations.

The rights and privileges of the free miners were confirmed by statute in 1838. Registered free miners still retained the sole right to gales from the Gaveller for mining coal and iron ore but now foreigners were able to secure title in law to gales and mine owners could employ whom they chose. By the middle of the 19th century about half the population of the Forest was employed at the coal works whilst the rest were working in the iron works or quarries or in the wood.

Richard Kear's ancestors had lived in the Forest of Dean from the 13th century, probably starting with Adam de Keyrlun who had come from Caerleon in Wales to Staunton around 1282 and who owned a forge there. The first definite mention of the name in one of its variants occurs in 1306 when Robert Keere of Tudenham(Tidenham) paid 2s.6d. per annum to the Lord of the Manor for $7^1/_2$ acres of land.[7] It would seem probable that many of the Kear families were engaged in agriculture in these early centuries as records show a great number of land transactions concerning meadows and pastures. By this time most of the Kears in the Forest of Dean had settled in Newland and Coleford. Newland, a village situated on the east side of the River Wye near Monmouth was the centre of a large parish of the same name with many settlements and complicated boundaries. The small village of Newland was centred round its 13th century church and was mainly residential. The centre of Newland parish was the market town of Coleford, which had developed round the junction of several roads and three brooks. It had no church of its own, but a chapel of ease was built during the 15th century. Next to Coleford were the villages of Bream and Clearwell and the hamlet of Whitecliff. Clearwell had one of the largest estates in the Forest of Dean having several large farms.

The Kears would have been tenants not owners of their land and it was not until the early part of the 17th century that Edward Kear was described as a yeoman. In 1603 Edward Keare yeoman of Breame and three others promised a payment of £40 next Ladyday to Dennis Compton, gent of Alvington and English Bicknor.[8] This Edward was the direct ancestor of young Richard Kear. Edward Kear was certainly a man of some importance as records show that he was a deputy gaveller and his will proved in 1613 shows that he had accumulated sufficient wealth to leave charitable bequests as well as large sums to his family. [9] Descendants of this Edward were almost certainly iron ore miners and in later years had important farming interests.

Throughout the 17th century the wealth of the Kears continued and the consequent status, which this brought, was reflected in the positions they held in the community. In 1673 a John Keare was a churchwarden at Newland for the Coleford tithing and in the same year it was recorded that Thomas Keare was Overseer of the poor of Coleford. The name of Keare appears in the court proceedings during the 1670s and 1680s as members of the jury and in 1676 a Richard Keare was one of twelve chosen from the Jury of forty-eight to consider which orders for management of the concerns of the 'Myners' could be revoked and which could remain.

Another sign of the status of the Kear families is shown by the size of the tombstones in the churchyard at Newland. The large tomb of Edward the

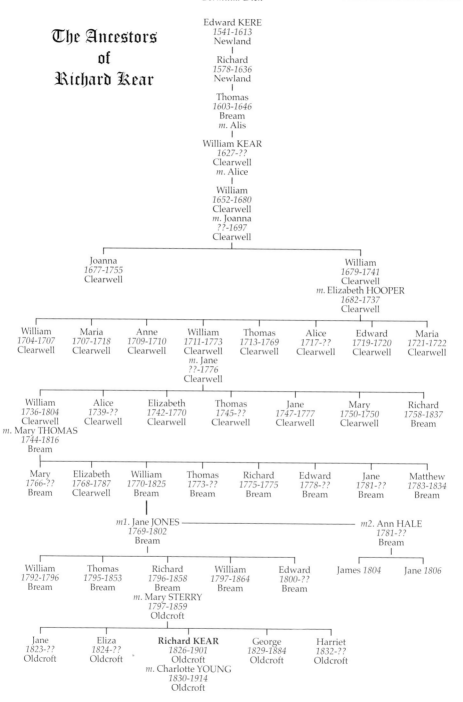

The Ancestors
of
Richard Kear

Edward KERE
1541-1613
Newland

Richard
1578-1636
Newland

Thomas
1603-1646
Bream
m. Alis

William KEAR
1627-??
Clearwell
m. Alice

William
1652-1680
Clearwell
m. Joanna
??-1697
Clearwell

Joanna
1677-1755
Clearwell

William
1679-1741
Clearwell
m. Elizabeth HOOPER
1682-1737
Clearwell

William
1704-1707
Clearwell

Maria
1707-1718
Clearwell

Anne
1709-1710
Clearwell

William
1711-1773
Clearwell
m. Jane
??-1776
Clearwell

Thomas
1713-1769
Clearwell

Alice
1717-??
Clearwell

Edward
1719-1720
Clearwell

Maria
1721-1722
Clearwell

William
1736-1804
Clearwell
m. Mary THOMAS
1744-1816
Bream

Alice
1739-??
Clearwell

Elizabeth
1742-1770
Clearwell

Thomas
1745-??
Clearwell

Jane
1747-1777
Clearwell

Mary
1750-1750
Clearwell

Richard
1758-1837
Bream

Mary
1766-??
Bream

Elizabeth
1768-1787
Clearwell

William
1770-1825
Bream

Thomas
1773-??
Bream

Richard
1775-1775
Bream

Edward
1778-??
Bream

Jane
1781-??
Bream

Matthew
1783-1834
Bream

m1. Jane JONES ———————————————————— *m2.* Ann HALE
1769-1802   *1781-??*
Bream   Bream

William
1792-1796
Bream

Thomas
1795-1853
Bream

Richard
1796-1858
Bream
m. Mary STERRY
1797-1859
Oldcroft

William
1797-1864
Bream

Edward
1800-??
Bream

James *1804*

Jane *1806*

Jane
1823-??
Oldcroft

Eliza
1824-??
Oldcroft

Richard KEAR
1826-1901
Oldcroft
m. Charlotte YOUNG
1830-1914
Oldcroft

George
1829-1884
Oldcroft

Harriet
1832-??
Oldcroft

yeoman who died in 1613 stands next to an even larger one in which several Kears who lived at Bream are buried including John Kear who, if we are to believe the tombstone, died in 1775 at the age of 107. Shortly after his death, records show the first Kear to be described as a gentleman. In 1785 a John Keare, gent, was among those on the Committee for the Coleford workhouse.[10]

By the start of the 18th century the number of Kear families had multiplied considerably with many of them still holding property and land throughout the Forest of Dean. The Kear wills that survive show that the family fortunes had been founded mainly on iron ore with farming as a sideline but gradually as the demand for coal increased later wills describe the Kears as colliers. In 1787 a survey for the Commissioners of Woods showing the ownership of gales in the Forest states that an Isaac Kear held five gales in Parkend Walk, Keir and Co. held three gales in Blakeney Walk and James and Benjamin Keer and Co. also had gales.[11] In 1790 a Benjamin Kear of Bream's Tufts left to his brother William his *'title belonging to coalworks in the Forest called the Royal Engine'*.[12] By the end of the 18th century it was calculated that there were ninety working pits in Dean and six hundred and sixty two free miners.

Richard Kear's grandparents, William and Jane, were married at Newland church on the 1st October 1791. Their first son, William, was born the following year and in 1795 their second son Thomas arrived. Richard came along next and he was baptised at Bream Chapel on the 16th February 1796. Sadly in the autumn of that year the eldest son, William, died but as was so often the custom of the day, when the next son was born in 1797 he too was given the name William. The final member of the family was yet another son named Edward, born in 1800. The baptism registers show that the family was living at Yorkley by this time. After his first wife Jane died, William, the grandfather, married for a second time. He married Ann Hale in 1803, and their first child was James born the following year. Their second child, William's only daughter, was named Jane, presumably after his first wife.

When Grandfather William died in 1825 he left a will,[13] signed with his mark, which gives a great deal of information about the status of the family. His wife Ann is not mentioned in the will so perhaps she pre-deceased him. He was living at the Tuft of Beeches near the Nagshead (Yorkley), and left two houses and land at the Tuft of Beeches to his three sons Thomas, Richard and William on condition that they paid £20 to Edward and Jane. He asked that his flock of sheep and cattle be sold to pay his debts mentioning one debt of £18 owed to his brother Edward. He left a clock to Richard and a bed and large oak table to Jane. His assets were given as being under £100.

The cottages that William left to his three eldest sons had been built on land owned by the Commissioners of Woods in an exchange from the Crown sometime before 1825. They overlooked Cut and Fry Green at Oldcroft near

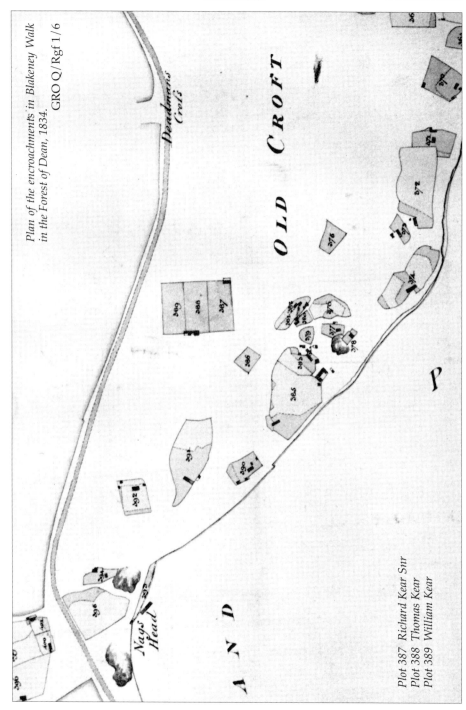

Plan of the encroachments in Blakeney Walk
in the Forest of Dean, 1834.

GRO Q/Rgf 1/6

Plot 387 Richard Kear Snr
Plot 388 Thomas Kear
Plot 389 William Kear

to the Nag's Head Inn. All three cottages and the land are shown on the Encroachment map of Blakeney Walk in 1834.[14] The land was equally divided into three strips of 2 rods and 18 perches each. An indenture dated the 4th January 1830 tells us that the three brothers built another cottage on the land at their own expense, which Richard Kear moved into. When Richard moved into his new house on the plot he also fenced a small area in front of his new cottage and in 1834 when the encroachment map was drawn up, he had to appear before the Commissioner of Woods to give evidence as to why he owned this small patch of land, measuring just one perch, which was extra to the land originally exchanged from the Crown. James Powell who was a close friend of the family and a keeper in the Forest gave evidence that Richard Kear had enclosed this area some four years before and so the Commissioners allowed him to keep the encroached parcel of land. Now each brother had a house on his own land.

Thomas, Richard and William probably worked in the coal mines from a very early age most likely at Parkend as the Kears had connections here. In 1802 an indenture was drawn up between Benjamin Williams of Monmouth, gent, and William Kear of Bream who was classed as a farmer and 'Pitt coal collier'. This was an indenture of co. partnership *'in the manufacturing of a Cindermount situate and being at a place called Park End in the Forest of Dean Gloucestershire for the purpose of making shot iron and Scruff'*.[15] In 1810 Isaac and Peter Kear set up a stamping mill for making glass from iron slag and in 1834 shows a James Kear owning seven acres of land and a house near Parkend furnace. The Parkend forges and coal pits were busy places as the Reverend Francis Witts described when he paid a visit to Mr. Machen, the deputy Gaveller, in 1836. He says that *'The principal forge which we passed is a gigantic grim mass of buildings, intersected by railway trucks, abounding in steam engines, frowning like some old timeworn fortress, whose huge dingy battlements resound with the clang of ponderous hammers, the blast of giant bellows, and similar impressive noises, now louder, now more suppressed, as the varied operations proceed'*.

Thomas Kear married first in 1816 at Newland church and brought his wife Harriet back to live at his cottage at 'Tuffettee Beach', which backed on to the Oldcroft enclosure. Next, William married Elizabeth Beddis at Awre in 1818. By 1836 William and Elizabeth had eight children and they moved to Littledean Woodside in East Dean. William still retained ownership of his cottage at Oldcroft and let it out to tenants until 1850 when he sold it to his nephew.

Richard Kear and Mary Sterry married in 1819 at Awre church down on the banks of the River Severn and came to live at Oldcroft in one of the two cottages. Two daughters Jane and Eliza were followed by a son born on the 20th November 1826. As he was the first son he was named Richard after his father, again a custom of the day. By the time the second son George was born in 1829 accommodation must have been getting a little cramped and it

Parkend Colliery.   Ian Pope collection

was then, in 1830, that Richard moved his wife and family into the new cottage built at the back of the three plots of land. In 1832 the last addition to the family came along, another daughter Harriet.

A survey of Oldcroft carried out in 1787 describes the area as '*for the most part covered with thorns, and hollys, with a few scrubby oaks and beech*'. By the time Richard junior was born most of the land in Oldcroft had been settled by encroachers except for Oldcroft plantation. In 1844 the plantation was fenced in three sections and an enclosure stone erected in each giving the acreage. In 1897 the three Oldcroft enclosures totalled 41 acres and were described by H. C. Hill as '*53 years old oak. Fair growth. Over thinned 4 or 5 years ago. Thrown open in 1896. Good quick fences exist around greater part, and it seems a pity to have opened it before having established an underwood of beech, which would have assured its future development*'. The old Dean road, which some believe to have Roman origins, runs from Mitcheldean through Deadmans Cross at Oldcroft to Lydney and was used by horses and carts right up to the early 1950s.

So it was in this small corner of the Forest of Dean that young Richard Kear with his two older sisters Jane and Eliza and his younger brother George and younger sister Harriet all spent their childhood. The Forest was described by the Rev. Witts in 1836 as '*undulating eminences of fine outline, one sweeping behind another, chiefly crowned with noble oak woods sequestered valleys of tangled copse, amidst which the birch and nut trees abound here and there a bare turfy hillside, with miners' cottages approachable by winding tracks and paths.'*

The cottage which Richard and Mary and their family lived in, which still stands today, was by Forest standards quite spacious, built of local Forest stone, with dirt floors. It had three rooms upstairs and two large rooms, one small room and a scullery downstairs. One of the rooms downstairs would have contained the clock left by young Richard's grandfather William. Outside in the garden every square inch would have been used. All the vegetables to keep a family fed were grown in the garden, which had a very secure wall or hedge round it to keep the Forest sheep out. Some families kept a few chickens, and holes were made in the boundary walls to allow the fowls free access to the green outside. Next to the outside privy, which was probably no more than a bucket or hole in the ground, was a thick stonewalled pig's cot. Most cottages in the Forest had a pig or two, fed on any scraps available including nettles and fern tops from the Forest and kelp from the banks of the River Severn. They were let out in the pannage season to forage for acorns on the green and a shout at night brought them back home. When they were killed it was quite a family event, the butcher was called in especially and after the pig was dead it would be laid onto a

The birthplace of Richard Kear, the property was originally all one cottage. These are plots 388 and 389 on the Encroachment map on page 8.   Averil Kear

pile of straw or fern, which was then set light to in order to burn off the hair. Every part of the pig was used including the bladder which when blown up made a football for the children to play with.

Many miners kept sheep, which by age-old privilege were allowed to roam free and graze in the Forest. The men who ran the sheep are known to this day as 'ship badgers', so called because of the way they 'badger' or remove another man's sheep when they find them grazing near their own. A 'sheep badger' may own two hundred sheep or just one ewe lamb and although he is an amateur the sheep are his capital and probably only property outside his small home. All the sheep would be marked with a sign such as a hand, a horseshoe or a heart. These ancient sheep marks were handed down from father to son going back to the times when the whole Forest was illiterate.

Between the cottage where young Richard lived and the Nag's Head Inn was Cut and Fry Green, which was grazed by sheep, pigs, goats and cattle in the mid nineteenth century. The mystery of the name Cut and Fry remains to this day with some preferring the theory that the miners would go into the local hostelry and cut a side of bacon to fry it, and some people who like the story that the exposed area of the green meant that a man could 'fry' in the hot summer sun or be 'cut' in half by the winter wind. By the time young Richard was born, his family had stopped keeping sheep preferring perhaps to spend all their spare time when not down the mines in religious pursuits.

Richard's mother had a hard time looking after her young family. Her time was spent providing meals for five hungry children and a coal miner husband. Washing was done in rainwater saved from the roof, there were metal grates in the cottage to be cleaned and Mary would have made sure the children were clean and tidy when they went to Sunday school. To help out the family finances some of the women would go bark scraping in the summer. Small pieces of bark were collected and then sold to the local tanneries where it was ground down into a powder used for curing leather. The Forest women also got good wages for birch stripping. The birch twigs were all cut to an even length and tied up into very small bundles with two bands round them like a besom. These were then taken to the clothing factories where they were used in the fulling process. The Forest of Dean at this time was a totally male dominated society, the men frequenting the many inns and alehouses in the area whenever they had the opportunity except on Sundays which were kept strictly for the family outings to church, chapel or in the case of the Kear family, the meeting house at Yorkley. There may have been limited schooling for the Kear children but Richard and his brother and sisters would have spent most of their days roaming the Forest collecting birds' eggs, climbing trees and building secret hideaways. They had to make the most of this short time because by the age of nine or ten the boys were sent off to work in the coal mines like their father. The girls were sent into service locally where possible or if not then in one of the big towns like Gloucester or Cheltenham. Some of the girls who were not sent away were forced to earn a small pittance by working alongside the men at the coal pits. They would have been at their posts in all weathers *'winding up the coal out of the shallow pits, some fifteen and twenty five yards deep, they did also load it into the carts and donkeys' bags and mules' bags'*.[16]

Richard Kear senior obtained his registration certificate to become a Free Miner in 1846 having worked a year and a day at Parkend Colliery just down the road. He gave his address as Tuft at the Beeches and made a mark in place of his signature. Many illnesses occurred due to the severe hardship of the mining work including bronchitis and rheumatic fever and of course there were the inevitable accidents. By 1851 Richard senior was a cripple and so presumably unable to continue in the pits making an even greater strain on the family income. His son Richard applied to become a Free Miner on the 28th June 1849 according to the certificate granted to him. On this he gave his place of residence as Tuft of Beeches and he signed his name at the bottom which meant that he had learnt to read and write. He was either taught at Sunday school along the road at Yorkley, or he and his brother and sisters may have occasionally attended the local school at Parkend, which had been opened in 1824.

In 1841 a book of poems was published, written by Catherine Drew in which she summed up the hardship of the Forest miner.

"You that in parlours warm yourselves enjoy,
By glowing fires, on a cold winter's day.
Think how the miners labour underground,
To aid you comforts in the crowded town.
And often times by accidents so sad,
They lose their lives, or limbs, and that's as bad;

Sometimes I've known a faulty rope give way,
And plunge them headlong from the light of day.
Yes, four and five at once, I've seen brought out,
A ghastly sight to see, you need not doubt,
Some lose their limbs, and some their precious eyes,
You human hearts, don't colliers despise,
Who underground their useful lives destroy,
While you enjoy the air, and light of day."

During the time that Richard Kear was growing up he made many friends, some good and some bad and many who were to play an important part in his story. The illegal sale of beer and cider meant that small beerhouses spread throughout the Forest ensuring that there was always one nearby

923

THE

ROYAL FOREST OF DEAN

AND

HUNDRED OF SAINT BRIAVELS,

IN THE COUNTY OF GLOUCESTER.

Application for Registration.

To the Gaveller and Deputy-Gaveller of Dean Forest.

PURSUANT to an Act passed in the First and Second Year of the Reign of Her Majesty Queen VICTORIA, intituled "An Act for regulating "the opening and working of Mines and Quarries in the Forest of "Dean and Hundred of Saint Briavels, in the County of Gloucester,"

I, *Richard Kear* of *Tuft of Beeches*

do hereby declare that I was born at *Tuft of Beeches*

Name and residence of Applicant to be here inserted in words at length.

in the said Hundred of Saint Briavels,

on the *twentieth* day of *November*

in the year of our Lord *one thousand Eight Hundred*

and Twenty seven and that I have worked a year and a

day in a *Coal Mine* within the said Hundred,

Here describe whether a Coal or Iron Mine, or a Stone Quarry, and also the particular Mine or Quarry.

that I am now abiding at *Tuft of Beeches* within the said

Hundred, and following the trade or business of *Coal Miner*

and I hereby claim to be Registered as a Free Miner, pursuant to the provisions of the above-mentioned Act.

As witness my hand this *28th* day of *June* 18*49*

Richard Kear

Witness,

George Morris Mase

Richard Kear's application for registration as a Free Miner in 1849. (His birth date is wrongly given as 1827, it should read 1826). GRO D5947 No. 923

14

where a miner could go after a hard day down the pit. The Elsom family lived in an alehouse in Yorkley called the 'Jovial Forester'. John Elsom had been a navigator on the river Wye at Llandogo and it was there that his son John and four daughters were born. Around 1845 John Elsom's wife Susanna died and the whole family moved to Yorkley. John junior soon became a coal miner at Parkend colliery where he met Richard Kear. One of John's sisters Mary Hathaway Elsom who was five years younger than Richard probably helped out in the alehouse before eventually moving to Gloucester into service. Richard was to meet up with her again much later.

Life was extremely hard for Foresters during the 19th century, there would not have been much time for socialising, except for visiting the local alehouse, so most friends would have been the people living nearby, work mates from the coal pits, and people who gathered together for religious meetings on a Sunday. The neighbours in Oldcroft, the James and the Charles families, all had children of the same age as Richard. George Charles was a labourer and James James worked with Richard in the pits at Parkend for a time. Both were to travel with him on the ill-fated journey to Bermuda.

Richard Kear had a large family so there was always someone around to talk to. By the 1850s all three of his sisters had married and produced families of their own, and he had many cousins both in the Oldcroft area and in Cinderford. By 1851 the Cinderford branch of the Kear family was becoming more educated and more affluent. Uncle William and two of his sons John

The small community of Oldcroft, Yorkley.   Ian Pope collection

and Thomas were colliers, another two sons were scholars and James, aged seventeen, was described as a tea dealer; working as an agent for a wholesaler Mr. Booth.[17]

On the 11th May 1850 Richard married Charlotte Young at Parkend church. Charlotte was born in 1830, the daughter of Nathaniel and Sarah Young who lived on Blakeney Hill. She had four sisters and two brothers and when she was just 11 years old she was sent out to work as a servant, living at the Red Hart Inn in the village of Awre. Charlotte's father, Nathaniel, died in 1844 leaving his house and lands on Blakeney Hill to his wife Sarah, with a clause that after his wife's death his sons should have the house and lands and his daughters should each receive £10. His will was not proved until 1853, by which time Charlotte would have been very grateful for the £10 that she received. After her marriage to Richard, Charlotte went to live with him in his parents' house at Oldcroft and almost exactly a year later on the 18th May 1851 their daughter Phoebe Ann was born. Richard must have thought that life was settling down well, but how wrong he was to be.

SOURCES
The sources used throughout this work appear at the end of each chapter; the abbreviations below are common to all.

BJAMH	Bermuda Journal of Archaeology and Maritime History
FOD	Forest of Dean
GRO	Gloucester Records Office
PRO	Public Records Office
VCH	Victoria County History

[1]   *VCH* Vol.V p. 285
[2]   *Ibid.* page 290
[3]   Hart. *The Free Miners.* (1st Edn.) p. 165
[4]   *Ibid.* p. 17
[5]   Research by Dr. Cyril Hart
[6]   Hart. *The Free Miners.* (1st Edn.) pp. 52-3
[7]   GRO Gloucestershire. Inquisitions post mortem. Vol. 5
[8]   GRO Compton papers D33/386
[9]   GRO 1613/?Edward Kere Will
[10] GRO P227 OV
[11] GRO D3921/IV8
[12] GRO Will 1790/132
[13] GRO Will 1825/?
[14] GRO GRgf 1/6 Encroachment map
[15] Gwent R.O. D25/1088
[16] Mountjoy. *The life of a Forest of Dean Collier.*
[17] Owen. *James Kear J.P.*

Chapter Two

RANTERS and RELIGION

Prison records show that Richard Kear gave his religion as 'Ranters'. It is certain that the teachings of this strand of Primitive Methodism were partly responsible for the actions which led to his imprisonment and subsequent transportation.

Richard Kear's ancestors had been well connected with the Church of England for generations with some of them becoming churchwardens and overseers to the poor. Concern by some of the Kears about the well being of poverty stricken Foresters is shown by the bequests left in their wills, as in the case of Edward Keare of Bream's Cross who, in 1613, left money to the chapel at Bream and to the poor of St. Briavels, Clearwell and Bream.[1] The Kears lived mainly in the area which was served by 'the Cathedral of the Forest', Newland Church. This church administered to a vast area and had two chapels-of-ease at Coleford and Bream and also the church at Clearwell. Devout men from these churches took their preaching to the Foresters in their own homes, and when these 'cottage lectures' had generated enough interest, new churches were built throughout the area. The Rev. Paylor Matthew Proctor, vicar of Newland, inspired the people of Berry Hill just outside Coleford, and in 1813 a church named Christ's Church was built there. In 1817 Holy Trinity Church at Drybrook was built by the hard work of the Rev. Henry Berkin, who was renowned for his compassion towards the poor and needy.

Another minister, Henry Poole, had been giving cottage lectures for some considerable time in the public house at Yorkley and he was concerned that the population of this southeast corner of the Forest had only the small chapel at Bream as a place of worship. In his application to the Bishop for a church to be built at Parkend he stressed how urgent it was *'Being thus unprovided with a place of worship and the means of public instruction, and following the corrupt dictates of their untutored minds, the natural consequences are a total neglect of all the duties of religion, accompanied with a prevalence of disorderly and immoral conduct'.*[2] Needless to say his application met with immediate response and in 1822 St. Paul's Church was built at Parkend together with a school *'for the instruction of the poor children'.*[3]

After the consecration of St. Paul's Church, John Horlick, an Independent minister in the Forest of Dean wrote, *'the people who worship in it, are greatly privileged, in having a gospel minister to break unto them the bread of life'*. It is also worth noting the description he gave of the surroundings at Parkend where young Richard Kear was living and working. *'The surrounding scenery in this part of the Forest of Dean though somewhat confined is exceedingly rural so that the spectator would be delighted with the pleasant umbrage and equally interested in taking a view of the collieries, likewise of the furnaces lately employed in melting iron'*.

Most people in the Forest of Dean were quite content to remain within the Church of England but early records show that the first wave of Nonconformity was growing by the time of the Restoration. In 1660 the Society of Friends were holding meetings at Coleford and Aylburton,[4] and Benfield House in Newland was licensed for worship by the Presbyterians in 1689.[5] In 1691 the house of James Baylis at Blakeney was licensed for worship by Protestant dissenters,[6] and the Independent movement was started in 1662 by a former curate of the Church of England who was unable to accept their doctrines. Towards the end of the 18th century the second wave of Nonconformist expansion swept through the Forest and the Independents and Baptists attracted large followings. By the beginning of the 19th century the Independents were the main Nonconformist denomination with some 82 meeting houses.[7] The antagonism of devout Anglicans towards all the early nonconformists can be illustrated by the case of Abraham Vaughan who in 1734 was *'charged upon oath on suspicion of breaking and entering the Meeting House in Mitchell Deane and also with pulling down the pulpitt and breaking several seats, and also with breaking several grave stones in the yard of the said Meeting House'*.

A comment on Nonconformity appears in the *Gloucester Journal* during the 1940s, which sums up the very English character of these breakaway religious sects. *'The Englishman's instinctive desire is to go out through doors labelled "Entrance" and to come in by doors labelled "Exit". The very word, Non-conformity, reveals a part of the secret. Its negativeness would have made it disheartening to anyone but the Englishman. He, however, exclaimed: "You tell me to* conform*? Like hell I will! I shall call myself a Nonconformist!" – and he suffered all sorts of things in the service of that chilly label. A good deal of their vitality left the Nonconformist sects when they began to insist on being called the Free Churches'*.

Richard Kear was a Primitive Methodist and this 'vitality' about religion was probably first encountered by his great-grandfather William who may well have attended the meeting at Coleford in 1739 when the Methodist, George Whitefield preached in the Market Hall to 100 people. Whitefield spoke vigorously about the new birth of souls and original sin, subjects which were bewildering to the Forest miners who were described in the early 1800s by the Rev. P. Proctor, the Vicar of Newland, as people who led unruly and disgusting lives with *'habitual profanation of the Sabbath-day, drunkenness, rioting, immodest dancing, revelling's, fighting's, an improper state of females on their marriage, and an absence and ignorance of the Holy Scriptures'*.[8]

George Whitefield was born in Gloucester in the year 1714. He had humble beginnings living with his mother at the Bell Inn and according to his own account he was a *'Sabbath-breaker, addicted to lying, filthy talking and foolish jesting'* although, there were occasions when he attended church. Living in Gloucester did, however, mean that he could attend the Free Grammar School where he went until he was fifteen. He then left school to help his mother run the inn for a year but the business did not do well and eventually she was forced to retire. Whitefield went back to the Grammar School to further his studies and he then went on to Oxford at the age of eighteen. Religion was beginning to become a very important part of his life and much of his spare time whilst at Oxford was spent visiting the local prison to read religious tracts to the inmates. While he was at Oxford he met up with the famous John Wesley and his brother Charles and a small group of young men who regularly discussed their religious convictions. They were soon given the name 'Methodists'on account of their strict 'method' of living. George Whitefield's Journal at this time says, *'I always chose the worst sort of food. I fasted twice a week. My apparel was mean. I thought it unbecoming a penitent to have his hair powdered. I wore woollen gloves, a patched gown, and dirty shoes; and though I was convinced that the kingdom of God did not consist in meat and drink, yet I resolutely persisted in these voluntary acts of self-denial, because I found in them great promotion of the spiritual life'*.[9]

John Wesley and his brother Charles joined by George Whitefield set about spreading their new found religion to all corners of the country. Whitefield was ordained in 1736 and gave his first sermon at the church of St. Mary de Crypt in Gloucester where he was born. Methodist Societies soon multiplied and in Bristol several groups were founded by John Wesley, who preached often to large crowds anxious to hear his words of hope for their salvation. Many churches refused to let John Wesley bring his new Methodism to their congregations and so, in an effort to reach all the poor people of the area he was often to be found preaching in the open. On one occasion a Bristol bowling green held a fervent crowd of five thousand. *'Blessed be God'* he said, *'that the bowling green is turned into a preaching place'* and he added *'I trust that assembly rooms and playhouses, those "strongholds of the Devil" will soon be put to similar use'*.[10] George Whitefield too, preached in the open air and became extremely popular with the mining communities around the Kingswood area of Bristol. In 1739 whilst preaching to a crowd of many thousands he says that *'The first discovery of their being affected was the sight of the white gutters made by their tears, which plentifully fell down their black cheeks as they came out of their coal-pits'*.[11] No doubt spurred on by his success in Kingswood Whitefield decided to bring his preaching to the Forest of

Dean. The coal miners here at this time were an insular race and very wary about accepting strangers into their midst so George Whitefield and his contemporaries found great resistance at first when they brought their new ideas to Coleford on the 9th April 1739. Whitefield's notes about that visit say *'Preached this morning in the Market-house at Coleford to about 100 people, and afterwards talked with effect to some scoffers at the inn'.*[12]

In 1740 George Whitefield separated from the Wesleys to follow his new interest as a Calvinistic Methodist, later known as the Countess of Huntingdon's Connexion from the patronage bestowed on them by that lady. He could not believe John Wesley's' teaching and wrote to him *'The more I examine the writings of the most experienced men and of the most experienced Christians, the more I differ from your notion about not committing sin'.*[13] The rift grew and ended with Whitefield blatantly preaching against the Wesley brothers. If Richard Kear had been alive in 1748 he would certainly have been interested to hear about the visit that George Whitefield made to Bermuda, as this was where Richard was to spend a great many years. Whitefield was met with great kindness in Bermuda and he says in his journal of the 17th May 1748 *'I have preached nearly seventy times; on week-days chiefly in private houses, but sometimes in the open air, to larger assemblies, they tell me, than were ever seen upon the island before. I have spent nine happy weeks among them, and was never so little opposed, during so long a stay in any place'.* He told of *'exceedingly fertile islands where vegetation is rapid, spring may be said to be perpetual; and fields and forests are clad with unfading verdure'.* Unfortunately in Richard Kear's circumstances he was not able to appreciate this beauty.

In 1749 Charles Wesley and his wife visited the Forest of Dean and had good reason to remember it. He had difficulty in finding lodgings in Coleford as it was the annual fair and when he tried to preach at St. Briavels he was stoned. By the time his brother John visited in 1756 a much kinder reception was recorded in Wesley's Journal. *'Monday, 15th March, 1756, we reached Coleford before seven, and found a plain loving people, who received the word of God with all gladness'.*[14] The people of the Forest of Dean were by now ready to enter into a different kind of religion, removed from the structure of the Church of England. By the time John Wesley paid his second visit to Coleford in 1763, Methodism was beginning to take hold as he writes *'The wind being high, I consented to preach in their new room; but large as it was, it would not contain the people, who appeared to be not a little affected, of which they gave a sufficient proof, by filling the room at five in the morning'.*[15]

After the death of John Wesley in 1791, several groups, all following their own particular beliefs and disciplines broke away from the original body of the Wesleyan Methodists. Despite the initial success of Methodism in the Forest of Dean, without John Wesley's zeal no great inroads were made until the early 1800s. If there were chapels in the Forest of Dean in the 18th century they were probably short lived as the Methodists were more concerned at that time with influencing other denominations rather than building churches of their own.

The Church of England had a great advantage over the Nonconformist bodies as it was already firmly established round the edges of the Forest and could obtain free grants for the purpose of building new churches and chapels. With the Nonconformists a minister or layman from an established meeting place outside the Forest, would start a cottage meeting for prayer and worship at some nearby place within the Forest. Converts would be made and when the group was large enough a new meeting house was formed. Many cottages were turned into meeting houses and travelling preachers from the chapels outside the Forest of Dean would come and preach regularly. In 1814 William Kear and three of his friends applied to the Bishop of Gloucester that *'the house of Jeptha James in the parish of Newland might be used as a place of worship by Protestant Dissenters'*.[16] This William Kear was at that time living at Bream, which is adjacent to Newland, and was probably young Richard's grandfather.

During this early part of the 19th century William Kear and his Wesleyan friends would walk to Redbrook on the banks of the River Wye for their Sunday worship. They all had a picnic lunch as the journey took a considerable time, and they met miners and their wives from South Wales who all held one dream of building their own Methodist Chapel.

Sometime in the early 1820s, Richard Kear's grandfather William moved to Oldcroft near the Nag's Head public house and joined the handful of Methodists who met in each other's houses. Some South Wales miners had moved into the Yorkley area and it was with their help that the first Wesleyan Methodist Chapel in the Forest of Dean was built at Whitecroft in 1824.[17] The choice of Whitecroft as a location for the new chapel may well have been due to the presence of a group of Independent worshippers who had met for many years in the shop of Samuel Baker. This shop at Whitecroft had been licensed for worship in 1787[18] just four years before the death of John Wesley when the Foresters were caught up in the fervour of new religions. The success of Whitecroft Chapel was almost immediate for it is recorded that *'in a few years following such a gracious work of God broke out that the Sanctuary was scarcely big enough to hold the congregation'*.[19] William Kear died in 1825 but his sons Richard and William held their father's strong Methodist beliefs and were able to have their children baptised at the new chapel by a visiting minister from the Monmouth circuit. Young Richard Kear was baptised on the 21st December 1826. His abode was given as Whitecroft, Parish of Newland and the occupation of his father Richard was given as 'collier'. Although Whitecroft chapel was not built until 1824, so strong was the faith of these early Forest of Dean Methodists that a cottage in Yorkley was witness to a Kear baptism in 1818 when Edward and Ann

Kear received the circuit minister to baptise their son Edward on the 12th November.[20] This Edward Kear was probably the occupier of the two perches of land next to the new Whitecroft Wesleyan chapel shown on the encroachment map of 1834[21] and this would make him young Richard Kear's great uncle.

Many of the Forest of Dean miners who had rebelled against the structure of the established church, and who were now finding the Wesleyan Methodists too formal, began to take part in cottage services, or attend out-door preaching offered by the Primitive Methodists. By 1820 some 202 travelling preachers were beginning to spread the word.[22]

This 'breakaway' sect really began to take a hold in the Forest of Dean when some colliers contacted the Primitive Methodist Circuit at Oakengates in Shropshire. One of the pioneers of Primitive Methodism on this circuit was John Roles who was currently preaching in Cwm, North Wales. He was appointed as missionary to the miners of the Forest of Dean and arrived in Pillowell in 1824. He worked much more exclusively among the poor and allowed greater influence to laymen within this sect. Even women were allowed to preach if qualified.

The original Whitecroft chapel built in 1824.
Averil Kear

In a short space of time a large circuit of cottages was established with Pillowell and Yorkley being included in one circuit with two travelling preachers to serve them. When each circuit grew so large that the travelling preachers could not visit them at least once a quarter they were divided to form yet another circuit and when enough money had been raised then a chapel was built. One travelling preacher named Richard Davies reported that the first chapel built for the Pillowell Primitive Methodist Circuit was at Lydbrook in 1828 and William Leaker when speaking about it in 1832 said that it was *'a triumphant day of prayer for Pillowell'* and went on to say *'from this time the Pillowell circuit became an important field of Primitive Methodist enterprise'*.[23] In 1835 Pillowell got its own chapel at a cost of £70, and in October 1836 a Richard Kear of Yorkley presented a certificate to the Bishop of Gloucester *'that a certain chapel situate at Yorkley and now in the holding of a congregation of Primitive Methodists, in the parish of Newland, is to be used as a place of religious worship'*.[24] This Richard was probably the son of Edward and Ann Kear who had been so active in setting up the Pillowell circuit some years before.

By 1850 Pillowell chapel had 41 members and Lydbrook chapel 32 members. The various cottage meeting places on the Pillowell circuit averaged about 12 members and records show that a meeting place at Oldcroft had 10 members in 1850.[25] This cottage at Oldcroft could well have been the home of Richard and Mary Kear and their family who by now were well entrenched in the Primitive Methodist cause. Their teenage sons Richard and George probably delighted in the popular notion that the 'Prims' were a rampaging band of rumbustious gospellers and did not mind the daredevil title of 'Ranters' which was given to them.

Young Richard Kear had been taught to read at the Sunday school organised by the lay preachers at the circuit meetings and it was here that he came across religious tracts and pamphlets, which were to shape his thoughts for years to come. One of the most famous Ranters was Abiezer Coppe who, in 1649, wrote a pamphlet entitled *'A Fiery Flying Roll'*. In this Coppe appeals very directly to the poor, saying that they *'will be raised up and earthly distinctions of title and property shall be done away with'*.[26] Coppe believed that God was sending him a direct message and described his actions as fulfilling God's instructions. He felt that he could show the world how he had been saved by blaspheming and constantly using the catch phrase 'Damn me, Ram me'. Coppe was thrown into gaol for his outrageous doctrines and a new act against blasphemy was passed. Another Ranter was Laurence Clarkson who avidly preached that God and the Devil were present in everyone and showing people that he had been saved by flouting conventional sexual morality. Clarkson wrote *' The Lost Sheep Found'* in 1660 in which he says the following *'Now I being as they said, Captain of the Rant, I had most of the principal women came to my lodging for knowledge, Now in the*

height of this ranting, I was made still careful for moneys for my wife, only my
body was given to other women: so our company increasing, I wanted for nothing
that heart could desire'.[27]

There is no doubt that the Ranters attack on social and moral order was taken to heart by the Forest of Dean Primitive Methodists and Richard Kear would have been no exception to this. He was a headstrong young man with a great zest for life. He loved his wife Charlotte and his little baby daughter Phoebe but still wanted to run with the pack. This all led to the shameful events of one day in July 1851. At the circuit meeting held at Pillowell chapel on the 15th September 1851 it was agreed that *'Oldcroft come off the plan',*[28] possibly because of the disgrace which Richard had brought to his father who was a leader at this meeting house, but more likely because even the Primitive Methodists with their strong religious views could not follow the outrageous beliefs of these 'Ranters'.

1   GRO 1613/47
2   Nicholls *Forest of Dean.* p. 168
3   John Horlick's manuscript GRO.
4   Bright. *The rise of nonconformity.*
5   GRO Q/SO 2 1689 Michaelmas
6   *Ibid.*, 1691 Michaelmas
7   GRO FD 11 p. 14
8   Nicholls. *Forest of Dean.* p. 156
9   Ryle. *Select sermons of George Whitefield.*
10 Ayling. *John Wesley.*
11 Ryle. *Select Sermons of George Whitefield.*
12 Stratford. *Good and Great Men of Glos. George Whitefield.* 1867. p. 239
13 Maldwyn-Hughes. *Wesley and Whitefield.*
14 Nicholls. *Forest of Dean.* p. 155
15 *Ibid.*
16 Owen. *James Kear J.P.*
17 GRO NC 80
18 GRO Q/SO2 Trinity
19 GRO NC 80
20 Gwent R.O. RG4/M52
21 GRO GRgf 1/6 Encroachment map
22 1851 Religious census reports
23 Lawrence. *Kindling the Flame.*1974.
24 Hockaday abstracts, GRO
25 Lawrence. *Kindling the Flame.*
26 Hughes. *17th century England- a changing culture 1618-1689.* 1984
27 *Ibid.*
28 GRO D2598 4/6

Chapter Three

CRY RAPE !

The events of Tuesday the 29th July 1851 were well documented in the local newspapers as a *'horrible outrage upon a woman'*. These reports were heavily biased towards the victim so we have no real way of knowing just how bad Richard Kear and his friends were, or indeed how pure the lady in question was. However, an incident certainly did take place that night which led to a whole new way of life for seven young men.

In 1851 Richard Kear was working as master of a pit at Oldcroft. He had worked with his father at Parkend colliery for a considerable time and it was there that he obtained his licence to become a free miner, but at some time prior to 1851 he was offered a job at one of the pits at Oldcroft owned by William Morgan and John Jordan. Old Croft Level colliery was situated about 50 yards south of the lower stone stile leading to Soilwell Farm, and the application for the gale in 1844 stated that *'there shall be wrought and gained in every year from Christmas 1846 a quantity of not less than 340 tons'*.[1] Morgan and Jordan were told to cease mining at this pit in 1848 as the coal produced was only suitable for coking and because the pit was so high up the smoke was damaging the trees. The two men ignored this order and carried on mining at Old Croft Level and at the other pits they owned at Oldcroft for some considerable time.

Richard was the chief wage earner by now as his father had become a cripple, probably due to long years in the pits, and so Richard not only had to provide for his wife Charlotte and their new baby Phoebe, but also for his parents and sister Harriet who all shared the cottage at Oldcroft.

On the evening of the 29th July Richard Kear went to the Nag's Head public house just across the green from his home for a club feast. Most of the Forest of Dean miners belonged to a benefit club of some kind called 'Odd Fellows', which provided funds for miners involved in accidents and sometimes enabled a widow to have a small sum if her husband was killed. There was a social side to these clubs, with many often having initiatory rites, mystic signs of recognition and secret ceremonies. Unfortunately many of these clubs were short-lived as *'so much of the contributions were spent in drink; then at their feast days they had a division of whatever they had above such a sum, and in that way they killed the goose that laid the golden egg'*.[2] That Tuesday

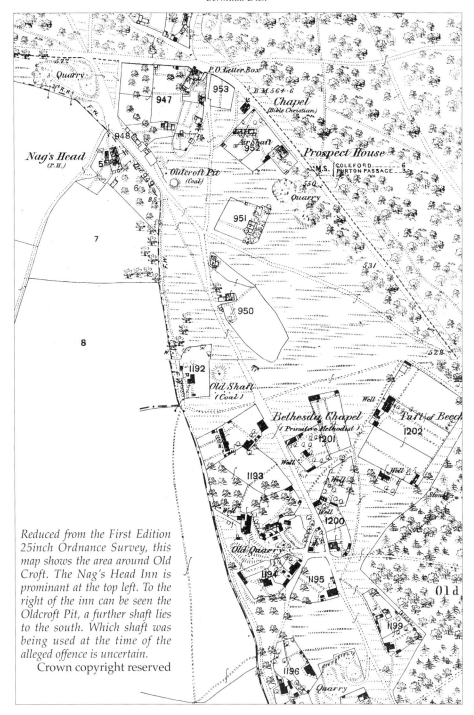

Reduced from the First Edition 25inch Ordnance Survey, this map shows the area around Old Croft. The Nag's Head Inn is prominant at the top left. To the right of the inn can be seen the Oldcroft Pit, a further shaft lies to the south. Which shaft was being used at the time of the alleged offence is uncertain.

Crown copyright reserved

The Nag's Head Inn, Yorkley.   Averil Kear

evening it was raining so Richard joined his friends inside the pub where the merrymaking and drinking soon justified the description given to Foresters as 'a sort of robustic wild people'.[3] The hardworking Forester was proud of his independence, suspicious of outsiders and fierce in the defence of his customs and when miners gathered together to drink in one of the many beerhouses in the area they could be quite an intimidating group. Music played an important part in the life of the Forester with brass bands and chapel choirs prolific throughout the area by the mid nineteenth century[4] and it is very likely that one of the favourite songs of the time would have been sung at the Nag's Head that evening.

'For we are the Jovial Foresters,
Our trade is getting coal;
You never knew a Forester,
But was a hearty soul'.[5]

George Charles, aged 23, lived at Oldcroft with his parents, brothers William and John and his sister Fanny. George was one of six labourers employed on the 200-acre farm at Alvington Court. The farm manager in 1851 was Thomas Williams and the land was mainly permanent grassland with some crops such as wheat, barley or turnips. Although George was not a coal miner, he too went along to the Nag's Head that evening for the club feast.

Thomas Stephens lived with his widowed mother Fanny at Oldcroft. He was 22 and for some years had worked for George Morse at the Wellington Colliery at Brandrick's Green. By 1851 he was working at Parkend Colliery, alongside James James who at the age of 19 had worked at Parkend for ten years. James came from a large family, with a father who liked his drink, sometimes too much as in 1845 when he was imprisoned in Littledean gaol for being intoxicated.[6] Both Thomas and James worked for David Gething, a colliery manager who after living in London for a while, had come to Parkend to manage one of the pits belonging to Edward Protheroe.

In 1841, the Parkend pits formed the biggest colliery in the Forest of Dean raising some 90,000 tons of coal in that year[7] and men and boys came from a wide area to work there. It was not unusual for boys as young as six or seven to be employed by unscrupulous mine managers eager for cheap child labour and of course most parents were forced by poverty to send their children into the mines. *'These child workers pulled trucks of coal along underground passages too narrow for grown men, or looked after ventilating doors under conditions that were very like solitary confinement in darkness'.*[8] Fortunately an Act was passed in 1842 which stopped the employment of women in the pits and children under the age of ten but this legislation was often ignored to suit both employer and impoverished families.

Hiram Archer started work at the Parkend Colliery at the age of 13. His mother Elizabeth was a widow who was forced to take in a lodger at their house in Pillowell just to make ends meet. Without any discipline from a father, Hiram was always in trouble and the night he visited the Nag's Head was no exception.

John Lee from Burnt Log near Moseley Green helped to support his family of four brothers and two sisters. He worked alongside his father at Parkend where he no doubt met fellow collier Thomas James who lived with his parents at Neats (Neds) Top Cottage at Oldcroft. Both Thomas and John were at the club feast on the 29th.

The last member of the group involved in events that night was Henry Shapcott. Henry's father Thomas was a tailor who, after leaving Bristol some time in the 1830s, had settled in Drybrook with his wife Ann and raised a family there. Henry left home and went into lodgings with Jonathan Hatton at Moseley Green along with two other men, Miles Morgan and Samuel Hale. Henry had been a collier for some time but in 1851 he was working for John Seaborne at Etloe on the banks of the Severn as an agricultural labourer.

Tramroads criss-crossed the Forest of Dean using horse-drawn wagons to carry the coal from the collieries down to the River Severn for onward shipment by sea or to join up with the new South Wales railway line, opened in September 1851 which ran along the banks of the River Severn linking Chepstow with Gloucester. The construction of the new railway line provided jobs for men from Wales and beyond and on the evening of the 29th July 1851, Mary McCarthy was walking from Coleford to Lydney in search of her brother who she knew was working on this line.

Mary McCarthy was born in Ireland in the early 1800s and came to London with her family to go into service. *'She lived in good families as a cook at Richmond, Kew and Twickenham but lost her character through having an illegitimate child'*.[9] After leaving London she went to Bristol where she earned her living through shopwork and selling caps. She lodged with a Mr. Barrett in New Street, Bristol and made him some shirts before he went off to America. She moved again to Cardiff and in 1851 she was living at Chepstow. She heard that her brother was in the area and she made her way slowly through the Forest asking people if they knew him. On her way to Lydney on that Tuesday evening the 29th July she felt unwell and the rain made her feel very cold. It was between nine and ten o'clock when she saw a glow coming from some charcoal braziers and she sat down to warm herself. She was very tired and thirsty and although she could hear revelry coming from the nearby pub she was too frightened to go in.

At about one o'clock Hiram Archer and James James left the Nag's Head and saw Mary sitting by the fire. They went over to her and she told them that she was not well and asked for a drink of water. The two men suggested that she would be warmer if she went into the pub with them and had a glass of beer, which they felt would be better for her, but Mary refused. Hiram told Mary that there was a pump in the yard of the pub and while she waited outside he went in and got her a drink of water.

In 1851 the owner of the Nag's Head Inn was William Charles[10] who also owned several other houses in Oldcroft and lived with his wife Elizabeth in a cottage attached to the pub. William was used to the high spirits of the miners when they had consumed vast quantities of beer and he often had to send for the local constabulary to sort out the inevitable fights which occurred. On the evening of the 29th July he once again had to send a runner down to Blakeney to fetch the police. Constables Ellison and Russell were called to the Nag's Head between half-past one and two o'clock to stop a fight, which had broken out, and Constable Ellison saw that Richard Kear had a cut on his face which was bleeding. They cleared everyone out of the pub and by the time Mary returned to the fire a small group of men were standing warming themselves. They were in a happy but belligerent mood after their night of drinking and general merrymaking and they laughed as they asked Mary if she felt better for the water.

There was a small cabin near the Nag's Head at the Old Croft Colliery

Pit and shack at Yorkley.

Ian Pope collection

and Richard Kear suggested that Mary should spend the rest of the night there as she was obviously not well. He told her that he was the master of the place with a key to the cabin and that if she went in then no one would interfere with her. Mary said that she would rather remain by the fire despite Richard Kear and George Charles trying to persuade her that she would be better inside. By now all the other men had gathered round and Richard and George asked Hiram Archer and James James to take Mary into the cabin. George threatened her by saying that she would be burnt in the fire if she did not go in, and he made her even more frightened by saying that another woman had been burnt there before.

Hiram and James took her by the arms and, according to Mary's statement, forced her into the cabin where they sat her between them on a form by the wall. George Charles brought in two shovels' full of the burning coke from the brazier outside which he placed in a small oven in the cabin shedding a soft light. He then left the cabin locking the door from the outside.

Mary was first raped by Hiram Archer whilst James James held her down and then it was the turn of James. They knocked on the cabin door and it was opened from outside. Next into the cabin was George Charles and after him Richard Kear, who as he left threw some ashes onto the fire which immediately darkened the place. Thomas Stephens went in next '*and on her remonstrating with him he said "Now hold your tongue; this shall be the last"*'.[11] Mary asked for a drink of water, which Thomas poured from a brown jug in the cabin and then he left. He was followed by Thomas James and, according to Mary's statement three other men who all committed the same offence. After the last one went out she sat down on the bench and waited for what might happen next. Thomas Stephens returned to the cabin and Mary begged him to leave her alone. He went outside and she heard him whispering to the others. After a few minutes Richard Kear went into the cabin and told Mary that she could stay there until seven o'clock and he would give her the key so that she could lock herself in. At this point George Charles rushed in brandishing a shovel which he held over Mary's head threatening to kill her if she did not leave, shouting as he did so that he would let Kear know who was master. A violent struggle followed and Richard finally managed to get hold of the shovel and push George away. During this Mary left the cabin and started to walk down the road. As she passed by the fire she noticed several men sitting by it and Thomas Stephens got up to join Richard and George who all began to follow her.

A short distance down the road Mary saw a house and staggered slowly towards it. George Charles and Thomas Stephens left the group but Richard Kear went up to her asking if she was hurt. He explained that he was a married man and would understand if she wanted to tell him where she was hurting. Richard probably did not consider that he had done anything wrong that night if he believed the teachings of the Ranters that God was

Two views of Westbury-on-Severn workhouse, 1969.

GRO GPS 354/2 courtesy Cyril Hart

within him and that therefore swearing and sexual freedom were not sinful. Mary brushed him aside and went on to the house where a Mrs. Ann Jenkins opened the door. Mary explained how shamefully she had been treated and the woman advised her to go to the police.

It was now about half past five in the morning and Mary continued to walk on until she came to a hayrick by the roadside at Nibley where she lay down unable to go any further. Ann Jenkins was worried about Mary and sometime during the morning she went down the road to see if there was any sign of her. On finding Mary by the roadside she offered her a drink of wine and went to fetch P.C. Ellison from Blakeney. After getting the necessary authority from the overseer of the poor of the parish of Awre P.C. Ellison placed Mary on a cart and took her to the Westbury-on-Severn workhouse some seven or eight miles along the road towards Gloucester. The master Henry Simons and his wife Mary Ann,[12] received her at the workhouse and at once called the surgeon Mr. Humble. He saw that she was suffering from a fever and was in a dreadful state, and immediately asked Mr. Simons to notify the police.

'*Information was at once given to the police at Newnham when Sergeant Hernaman with Constables Russell, Ellison and Gleed, at once left in quest of the offenders*'.[13] Richard Kear and Thomas Stephens were arrested on the 1st August 1851 and taken directly to Littledean House of Correction near Cinderford. James James was taken to Littledean on the 2nd August and George Charles on the 4th. The police then set about finding the other suspects as Mary McCarthy had stated that nine men in total had raped her that night. It was not until the beginning of September that Henry Shapcott and John Lea were finally arrested. When they were brought before Mary McCarthy at the Petty sessions at Newnham she '*immediately identified Shapcott as one of the men who brutally assaulted her, and she said Lea was also present but she could not say whether he had ill treated her in the same manner as the others*'.[14] The *Gloucester Journal* reported the arrest of yet another man at Blaenavon in Wales. '*We have now to announce the apprehension of another collier on the same charge named Hiram Archer, residing at Pillowell, who had absconded on the morning after the outrage. Mary McCarthy positively identified the prisoner as the man who first committed the offence upon her*'.[15]

The news of '*The brutal outrage in the Forest*'[16] spread from house to house and filled the newspapers for many weeks. Even the *Times* in London heard about it and one reporter was so moved by the story that he sent some money for the welfare of Mary McCarthy. Henry Simons the master of the workhouse sent a letter of thanks, which was reproduced in the *Gloucester Journal* on the 23rd August 1851.

'THE CASE OF RAPE AT WEST DEAN GLOUCESTERSHIRE.

To the Editor of the Times.

Sir- I received this morning a letter per post from your powerful correspondent, the Hon and Rev. S. Godolphin Osborne stating that he had read the report of the trial of the above case in your column of Saturday, enclosing a cheque for £2 for the benefit of the ill-used woman. As this case is, I believe, second to none on record in brutality and real suffering and the woman is sensible, intelligent and well-conducted I have ventured to send these few lines to you'.

The letter continues with details of the character and employment of Mary McCarthy and ends by saying, '*Should you be pleased to insert this letter in your valuable journal it may be of considerable benefit to the poor woman'.*

Of the nine men accused of rape by Mary McCarthy on that Tuesday night of the 29th July 1851, seven had now been detained in Littledean House of Correction and one by one they were taken to the Court at Newnham to hear what fate had in store for them.

[1]   GRO D5947/3/2 Gales granted by the deputy gavellers of the Dean.
[2]   Mountjoy. *The Life of a Forest of Dean Collier.* p. 52
[3]   *VCH,* Vol. V. p. 381
[4]   *Ibid.,* p. 382
[5]   *Lydney Observer* 25.12.1925
[6]   GRO Q/Gli 16/5 no. 280
[7]   Anstis. *The Story of Parkend.*
[8]   *Ibid.,* page 27
[9]   *The Gloucester Journal* 23rd August 1851
[10]   GRO Will 1856/175
[11]   *The Gloucester Journal* 14th August 1851
[12]   1851 Census returns
[13]   *Gloucester Journal* 20th September 1851
[14]   *Ibid.,* 27th September 1851
[15]   *Ibid.*

Chapter Four

NEVER CONVICTED BEFORE

After Richard Kear was arrested, he and the other prisoners were held at Littledean House of Correction whilst awaiting trial at the Petty Sessions court at Newnham. They were not kept there for very long but this was to be the first prison of many they were to see over the next ten or twelve years.

Before the end of the eighteenth century prisoners in the Forest of Dean who had been convicted of petty crimes were held at St. Briavel's Gaol for debtors which belonged to Lord Berkeley. Here, there was one room for men and another for women, no allowance was provided for food, there was no area for exercise and no warmth in the winter. Ventilation in many of these old bridewells was severely lacking causing serious outbreaks of gaol-fever, which during the 1780s resulted in many deaths. By 1783 a report about these dreadful conditions had been passed to Sir George Onesiphorus Paul who immediately began large-scale reform of the prison system in Gloucestershire. Some old bridewells, the name derived from an ancient spring 'the Bride's Well' near a London prison,

Littledean Prison.   Ian Pope collection

The inside of Littledean Prison.   courtesy John Saunders

were replaced and completely new ones were built, including one at Littledean near Cinderford.

The building of Littledean Prison started in 1788, it was built on a foundation of cinders left over from the site of old iron workings. It had red sandstone walls and the roof was covered with slates fixed by locally made nails. It had four courtyards, a chapel, and the main building containing the keeper's room on the first floor from which he could oversee the exercise yards. Two cell wings led off the main building, each identical, having day cells on the ground floor and eleven night cells on the first floor together with a dark cell for punishment. These cells were well ventilated and contained a cast-iron bedstead with covers, which were changed monthly. Littledean had been built to house 24 prisoners. The first one arrived in November 1791 but by 1795 there were only three prisoners and between 1798 and 1803 hardly any prisoners were admitted.[1] This lack of inmates to carry out basic jobs of work meant that for many years the expenditure of the prison far outweighed the income provided by the work of the prisoners.

A sudden increase in the numbers of inmates to 27 in 1805 resulted in the prison paying its way once more and this trend continued with 84 prisoners passing through Littledean in 1817.[2] Most prisoners only served one month in a house of correction as many serious offenders were sent on to Gloucester Gaol. The original intention for the houses of correction to help reform offenders was therefore difficult as none were detained in Littledean long enough to be taught a useful trade. The numbers continued to increase with the *Returns from all Gaols, Houses of Correction*[3] etc. showing that in 1820, 109 prisoners passed through Littledean, with the greatest number held at any one time of 28.

A new prison at Pentonville was built in 1842 to very high standards, which were copied throughout the country. It was thought that a regime of solitary confinement would be best for prisoners to stop them being mislead by other inmates and supposedly reform them completely. Cells were to be designed with good lighting and ventilation with toilet facilities in each, which would allow for the prisoners to work and sleep without the 'contamination of others'.[4] The chairman of the county bench did not go along with this idea of separate cells for each prisoner as he felt that some of them needed human contact to keep their sanity. He also felt that only minor trades such as shoemaking and mat making could be carried out in such confined rooms instead of the heavy work on the handmill and the treadwheel. Although there was a move by the Committee of Inquiry into Prisons to close Littledean House of Correction the chairman of the bench in Gloucestershire complained that this would mean prisoners being sent to Northleach, some 30 miles away and it would force police stations to become small prisons without any proper rules or supervision. There were no facilities at Gloucester Prison for housing petty criminals and to build a new prison especially for this purpose would be extremely costly. It was finally agreed in 1844 that Littledean should undergo several major alterations based on the Pentonville model.

There were now to be three distinct areas in all houses of correction, a 'no labour' area, for prisoners who were waiting for a few days before being removed for trial, a 'hard labour' area, for those in prison no more than three months before release, and a ward for females. The sixteen men's cells on the ground floor were all enlarged from 7ft. 8in. by 5ft. 8in. to 12ft. 6in. by 5ft. 9in. Each had a toilet and washbasin, a hammock for sleeping, and a table and chair. The cells upstairs were not enlarged but had heating installed. There were only four cells for female inmates, but these too were altered in the same way. The main area of the prison was also altered with two infirmaries added to the upper floor and a schoolroom and chaplain's room to the ground floor.

In 1850, just before Richard Kear and the others arrived, new record books were introduced which allowed the visiting magistrates to have a clear picture of the health and conduct of each of the prisoners. The new books included Account books, Clothing, Prisoners' Property, Punishment, Labour, Chaplain's and Schoolmaster's records. Of course, the smooth running of Littledean Prison depended largely on the officers running it and in 1847 the visiting magistrate was forced to note that the staff were constantly drunk and absent without leave. He discovered that the keeper William Haviland had employed prisoners in his own garden, had allowed the male and female prisoners to talk to each other and had allowed his journal to be filled in with notes made by the turnkey. The magistrate finished by writing in his minute book '*We strongly recommend that they should be removed as soon as possible'*. The matter was discussed at the Easter Quarter Sessions and the result was the instant dismissal of the keeper and his wife, the turnkey, porter and schoolmaster.[5]

A new keeper was appointed in March 1847 by the name of Thomas Shepherd, he was an ex- police sergeant aged 25. His job as keeper paid him an annual salary of £75, and he also took on the job of schoolmaster with his wife Maria employed as matron and schoolmistress. Richard Bennett became the new turnkey or hard labour man and Joseph Morris was employed as porter and day guard. It was obviously thought necessary for Thomas Shepherd to be given some instruction in prison discipline, probably due to his inexperience, for in December 1847 he was sent to Gloucester Gaol for two days training.[6] He was issued with new rules stating that the keeper should not be absent for more than two hours a day and should note the reason for this in his journal. He was to keep a record of all leave given to his staff and should not allow more than half the officers to be on leave at any one time.

Richard Bennett, the turnkey, was not a well man and eventually resigned in 1849, when Edward Beard who had been the turnkey at Littledean in 1845 took his place. Beard had been dismissed in May 1845 as his services then were no longer needed, and he saw the other side of prison life in September of the same year when he was imprisoned for two weeks for assault.[7] Obviously the small matter of a criminal record was no bar to once again obtaining the job of turnkey in 1849 but it is more likely that he was taken on as there were no other applicants for the job. Edward Beard was the hard labour man at the time Richard Kear and the others arrived but would not have had much contact with them as they were there for such a short time.

Richard Kear would have known a great deal about the inside of Littledean House of Correction as his younger brother George had been sent there in 1847. George Kear was just 18 when on the 13th of May 1847 he assaulted police sergeant Thomas Webb at Awre. At the Petty Sessions his sentence was to pay £20.14s.4d. or to serve two calendar months hard labour. There was no way that any of the Kear family could afford such a large sum of money and the prison register shows that George was admitted to Littledean on the 10th June 1847.[8] It also gives a description of George Kear as being 5ft 7in. tall weighing 11st. 9oz., dark brown hair and blue eyes, with a round face and clear complexion. In these days before photography an accurate description was very important and it even noted that George had a cut on his chin and a cut on the 'rist' of his right hand. His occupation was given as a collier and his abode as Deadmans Cross, West Dean. The remarks column stated that he 'has a father and mother, one brother and three sisters'. He was of *'pretty good character, seldom attends any place of worship and is connected with very bad characters'*. The register entry ends by saying that he was *'never convicted before'*.

The prisoners' property book showed that George was wearing one waistcoat, one pair of trousers, one shirt, one pair of stockings, one pair of boots, one hat, one pair of braces and a smock. He carried two handkerchiefs, 2d. in money and one song.[9] This song or 'chapbook' that George Kear had with him might have been one of the 'small godly books' given to him by the preacher in the local chapel. These godly chapbooks would have been instructional or catechismal manuals, which stressed the role of the family in religious education and usually contained morning and evening prayers. However, as the prison register showed that George hardly ever went to chapel, it is much more likely that he had one of the 'small merry books', perhaps bought surreptitiously or passed on to him by a friend. It is not difficult to imagine that the twopenny print stressing marital and extra-marital intercourse, or cuckoldry, as themes may have been very popular in the mining community of the Forest of Dean. George would certainly have felt very grown-up and wicked carrying one of these stories.

Punishment for George Kear whilst he was in Littledean would have been either breaking stones into gravel, cutting wood or working the treadwheel. Seven men at a time would turn the treadwheel at 48 steps a minute for nine hours a day in the summer and seven hours a day in the winter. It had no real benefit except as exercise, which left the prisoners so hot that the guards made them walk round the yard to cool off after coming off the wheel. It was probably during one of these sessions in the yard that George had a fight with Henry Paradise. The prisoners' punishment book shows that they each had one meal of gruel stopped *'for sparring at each other and making a noise in the yard'*.[10] The continuous diet of gruel, bread and watery soup meant that most of the prisoners suffered from diarrhoea and George was no exception. The Medical Officer's Journal shows that he had 'acidity of the stomach and bowels' or 'dyspepsia' for a week in June and in the same month the Medical Officer recommended *'the Governor to have some mint tea made for the men to drink who are employed on the treadwheel'*.[11]

Henry Willis, the chaplain in 1847 was responsible for showing the men the error of their ways and to give them religious instruction. His journal and prisoners character book stated that George Kear could not read very well on admission but he could recite the Lord's Prayer, the Creed and the Ten Commandments. On the 9th August Henry Willis wrote in his journal about George *'Can read a great deal better and is greatly improved in religious knowledge. Gave him a bible'*.[12] The following day, the schoolmaster too, noted that he was very pleased with the progress of George's reading and writing. A comment by the keeper Thomas Shepherd at the same time remarked *'prisoners well behaved and most of them anxious to learn'*.[13] George's overall conduct in prison was given as 'very good'. A letter was sent to George's father Richard at Oldcroft informing him that his son was to be discharged on the 10th August at 9 am.

Shortly after his discharge George Kear became the first of his family to move

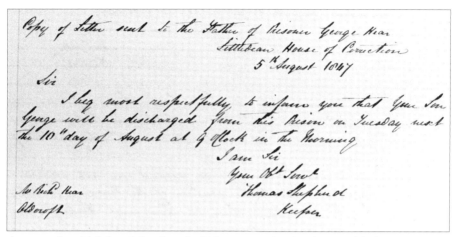

An extract from Littledean Prison letter book No. 13, 1847 showing the copy of the letter concerning the release of George Kear. GRO Q/Gli 4

to foreign shores when he emigrated to America. He settled first in the mining community of West Salem Township, Mercer, Pennsylvania where many Forest of Dean miners found employment. It was here that George met and married Lowetta Williams in 1851. George heard that new mining ventures had been started in the state of Illinois and during the 1860s he and his wife moved to the small town of Sparland where they raised thirteen children. The Methodist upbringing that George had received in the Forest of Dean could be continued in this new environment as a fine Methodist church had been built at Sparland in 1857. The Kear family settled comfortably in their new home, seeing the development of coal mining, the building of a paper mill and a distillery. The adjacent town of Steuben had provided George with employment at the mine of the Steuben Coal Company but by 1871 work here was suspended and George moved to new workings at Sparland where plentiful good quality coal was produced. George died in 1884 but it is doubtful if any of his family in the Forest of Dean ever knew what happened to him.

On the 1st August 1851 Richard Kear and Thomas Stephens arrived at Littledean prison to await trial at the Petty Sessions court at Newnham. Richard was described as being 24 years old, 5ft. 9in. in height, having brown hair, grey eyes, and a long face with a fresh complexion. The prison register also noted that he had a cut on his left nostril and that at sometime his left leg had been broken. His occupation was given as a collier and the cause of his commitment was that '*on 30th July 1851 at West Dean he did unlawfully assault and carnally know one Mary McCarthy and did feloniously ravish her, contrary to the form of the statute*'.[15] The remarks section stated that he was a married man with one child living at Yorkley, and had never been convicted before.

Thomas Stephens, who was admitted on the same day, was described as a man of 21 being 5ft, 2¹/₂ in, tall with brown hair, 'hazle' eyes and a scar across the bridge of his nose. His occupation was given as a collier and the remarks stated that he lived with his mother at Yorkley and had never been convicted before. Next to be caught was James James, who was admitted to Littledean on the 2nd August. He was 5ft. 2¹/₂ in., brown hair, 'hazle' eyes, a round fresh face and an old burn down his left cheek. The cuts and burns from which the coal miners suffered looked black and blue even after the wound had healed as coal dust impregnated their faces all their lives. James James like Richard Kear would have known about imprisonment in Littledean as both his father in 1845 and his elder brother George in 1849 had been held there for a while. In 1851 the prison register shows that James James lived at home with his father and mother, had always worked in the coal mines and had never been convicted before.

On the 4th August 1851, George Charles was arrested and taken to Littledean. He was 22 years old and his home was Oldcroft. He was described as a farmhouse labourer and the remarks said that he *'has lived at service this 10 years'*. George had brown hair, grey eyes and was 5ft. 2¹/₂ in. tall. He had a round fresh face with a scar across his nose. The register also noted that he *'has relations of indifferent character, and had never been convicted before'*.

On arrival at Littledean a note was made of the articles of clothing which each of the men wore together with any money and other miscellaneous articles. These first four men all carried tobacco with them and a few coppers apart from George Charles who was noted as having a knife and a watch and 2s. 6¹/₂d. in money. Although they were only in this prison for four days they were all given a medical check and weighed. A record was kept of any disease they had and their general condition on admission. All four men were given a clean bill of health and their weights were given as Richard Kear 11st. 2lb., Thomas Stephens 8st. 12lb., James James 8st. 9lb. and George Charles 10st 1lb.[16] As they were being held on remand for such a short time they were not involved with the routine of prison work but they did have to attend instruction by the prison chaplain Mr. Willis who explained a portion of the catechism to them every day.[17]

The County Court met in the town hall at Newnham on *'the Friday next after the first Monday in each month'*,[18] and it was here that these first four men to be arrested were brought on the morning of the 5th August 1851. The attending magistrates on that day were Sir Martin Hyde Crawley Boevey and Edwin Owen James, men of great standing in the community who were determined to make an example of the men standing before them. Mary McCarthy was considered to have recovered enough to be brought by cart from the workhouse at Westbury-on-Severn to identify the men whom she alleged had assaulted her.

At the time of this first trial at the Petty Sessions Mary stated that after five out of the nine men had committed the offence, the fire was put out, so that she was unable to identify more than five men, one of whom had not yet been

THE PRISONERS'

Date. 1851	Name.	Bed.	Blankets.	Coverlets.	Sheets.	Coats.	Waistcoats.	Trousers.	Drawers.	Shirts.	Stockings.	Shoes.	Boots.	Hats.	Gaiters.	Braces.	Handkerchief.	Smock-Frocks.	Knives.	Watches.
28 July	Thomas Jones					1	1		1	1	1		1	1		3				
1st Aug	Rich.ᵈ Bear					1	1	2	1	1		1		1	1				
1st do	Thomas Stephens					1	1		1	1		Cp		1					
2nd do	James Adams					1	1		1	2	1		Cp		1	1			
4 do	Geo. Charles					1	1	2	1	1		1		1	1			1	1
12 do	James Dance						1	1		1	1	1		Cp		1	1		
12 do	John Besser					1	1	1		1	1		1		1	1			
13 do	Benj.ⁿ Wheeler					1	1		1	1		Cp		1	1	1			
16 do	John Kinna					1	1	1		1		Cp		½					
16 do	George Bliss					1	1		1	1		1		1	1				
21 do	Thomas Scrivens					1	1		1	1		1		1	1	1			
21 do	William Price					1	1	2	1	1		1		1	2	1			
22 do	James Dance					1	1		1	1		Cp		1	1				
23 do	Henry Barton					2	1		1	1		Cp		1	1	1			
25 do	James Dance					1	1		1	1		Cp		1	1				
25 do	James Bigglestone					1	1	1		1		1		1	2		1		
26 do	William Cooper					1	1		1	1		1		1	1	1	1		
8 Sep	George Thomas					1	1		1	1		Cp		1	1	1			
10 do	James Adams					1	1		1	1		Cp		1	2	1	1		
16 do	John Davis					1	1		1	1		1		1	1				
17 do	Henry Shipscott					1	1		1	1		Cp		1	1				
17 do	John Sea					1	1		1	1		1		1	2		1		
18 do	Hiram Archer					1	1		1	1		1		1	1				
20 do	Charles Roberts			✗	1	1		1	1	1		Cp		1	1	1	1		
20 do	George Davis				1	1		1	1	1		1		1	1	1	2		
29 do	Thomas Smith			✗	1	1		1	1	1		Cp		1	1				
29 do	George Davis				1	1		1	1	1		1		1	1	1			
29 do	William Puen				1	1		1	1	1		Cp		1	1	1			
4 Oct	John Lewis				1	1		1	1	1		1		1	1				

Michaelmas Sessions 1851

[signature]

Littledean Prison, prisoners' property book. GRO Q/Gli 11/1

PROPERTY BOOK.

Little Dean Ho of Correction 71

Money.		Miscellaneous Articles.	By what authority restored, or given, or applied for by Prisoner.	Date when restored.	Remarks.
s.	d.				
14	7	Key	Given on Discharge	27 Aug.t	
	1	Tobacco	Do	5	
	5	Tobacco	Do	5	
		nothing	Do	5	
2	6½	Tobacco	Do	6	
		none	Do	19	
1	4½	none	Do	1 Sep.t	
2	8	Tobacco & pipe	Do	18 Aug.t	
		none	Do	20	
		none			
		Key	Do	25 Aug.t	
6		Key — Letters	Do	25	
		nothing	Do	25	
1		nothing			
		nothing			
		nothing	Do	26 Aug.t	
		nothing	Do	10 Sep.t	
		none	Do	7 Oct.	
	4	none	Do	7 Oct	
		about 1 lb of Cheese	Do	1 Sep.t	
		none	Do	10 Sep.	
		none	Do	18	
		none	Do	22	
1	10½	Letters & a Ring	Do	3 Oct	
		Comb	Do	3 Oct	
		none			
½		Apple Soap &			
5½		none	Do	5 Oct	
		Bill & Tobacco Box			

[signature]

apprehended. She then positively identified Richard Kear, James James, George Charles and Thomas Stephens. A journalist from *The Monmouthshire Merlin* was in the courtroom and reported that '*this is one of the worst cases of the kind that has happened for many years, and appears to have been perpetrated with the greatest determination, by wrestling and overpowering the woman until she lay almost lifeless, and it is astonishing that her senses should have survived so long under such revolting circumstances*'.[19] The magistrates then committed all four men for trial at the ensuing Gloucester assizes, and they were immediately removed to Gloucester Prison.

Henry Shapcott was entered in the register at Littledean as 'Shipscott'. He and John Lea were brought to Littledean on the 17th September and Hiram Archer on the 18th. Shapcott and Lea obviously thought that they were innocent of any crime as they stayed in the area and carried on with their work until their arrest, but Hiram Archer who Mary had said was the first man to commit the 'outrage', had run away and only just been found by police in Blaenavon. Once again the prison registers give a clear description of all three men. Henry Shapcott, who sometimes used the name Pride as an alias, was a collier living at Drybrook, near Ruardean with his widowed mother. He was 18 years old and stood at 5ft. 4in. He had brown hair, grey eyes and his mouth was deformed. He had always worked in the coal mines and had never been convicted before. John Lea at 19 years old and 5ft. 3 1/2 in. had black hair, grey eyes and a long face with a dark complexion. He lived at Burnt Log, East Dean and he and his father were both colliers. He had never been convicted before.

It was no wonder that Hiram Archer had tried to evade capture, he was the only one of the men who had a previous conviction. For ten days in September 1844 Hiram had been held in Littledean House of Correction for absenting himself from his master's service. At the time of this first conviction the remarks in the prison register showed that he had a very good character. The property book showed that apart from the clothes he had on, he carried one tobacco box and the schoolmaster's journal noted that he could neither read nor write but was very attentive in class. Hiram Archer was given a sentence of ten days hard labour, breaking stone to '*repair the Road leading from the Queens highway to the Bridewell*'.[20] This was back breaking work for 18 year old Hiram, even though he was a collier, but his family did not desert him, as the prison register remarks that '*the mother of this prisoner called to know the day of liberation*', and she was given '*the date and hour on a piece of paper*'.[21]

By the time Hiram Archer came to Littledean for the second time the prison register tells a very different story as he is then described as being of 'very bad character'. Now at the age of 26 his description is given as 5ft. 2in. tall with black hair, dark eyes and a long dark face pitted very much from smallpox. He was an inhabitant of Yorkley and a collier.

Shapcott, Lea and Archer were all noted as wearing ordinary clothes, John Lea had a knife and none of the men carried any money. They were all noted as being in good health on admission and their weights were noted as Shapcott 8st. 10lb., Lea 8st. 2lb. and Archer 8st. 5lb. A new diet was introduced into Littledean Prison on the 1st August 1851 which increased the portions of bread and gruel given to each prisoner and for the first time gave an allowance of 9oz. of meat and 6oz. of rice every day.[22] This new diet may have been the first good food that these men had eaten for some considerable time which may have given some comfort to them whilst waiting to hear their fate.

The day after these three men were arrested, they were taken from Littledean to Newnham for trial at the Petty sessions court. Once again Mary McCarthy was brought in and on oath repeated the story she had told before, reiterating *'I was not in any quarry that night before I went to the fire, and I did not get any money that evening from any man'*.[23] She then identified Hiram Archer as the man who first assaulted her. The magistrates only had time to hear the evidence of two of the men that day, and as Hiram Archer had only just been apprehended, he was held over for trial until the following Monday.

Mary McCarthy then went on to give details about Henry Shapcott who she said she remembered very well. Her statement read, *'he was dressed in the clothes that he is wearing now. I remember the jacket. I saw him sufficiently at the fire; it was so light I could see to thread a needle. I know his face. I knew him directly when he was shewn me by the policeman. When Shepcot came into the cabin and assaulted me, I was on the floor, and cried out but not so strong as I did before. He pulled me about but never spoke. The fire did not give so much light as it had before, and I was getting weak and could not take so much notice; but I could see the man's face and his jacket, and it was the prisoner next to me Shepcot'*.[24]

John Lea was then brought forward for identification but Mary could only say about him that she had seen him by the fire at the time a man had brought her water by the gate of the public house. She went on to say that *'If Lea came in at all, he came in next to the one who kicked me, but I was very low, and I cannot swear so hard at him as I can at the other. He was dressed I think in a jacket, a blue round one, and a cap.'*

Several witnesses were brought into the court to give evidence on behalf of John Lea and Henry Shapcott. The first was Samuel Hale who stated that he left the Nag's Head Inn about one o'clock in the morning, and went home with Henry Shapcott, Miles Morgan and John Lea. Samuel Hale said that they all lived at Moseley Green except John Lea. When they reached Moseley Green, which is about two miles from the Nag's Head, John Lea went on his way towards Burnt Log where he lived. Hale went on to say that there were still about fifty men at the inn when he and the others left, but neither he nor his friends had been to the coke pit where the incident took place. Stephen Joy was sworn in next and also stated that he went home with Lea and the others and that none of them went to the coke pit. Miles Morgan, too, said that he and the others arrived home at Moseley Green at about 2 o'clock in the morning. John Lea's father James was next called to give evidence and he said *'the prisoner*

John Lea is my son; he came home about half past three o'clock in the morning of the 30th July'.

Jonathan Hatton was next called as a witness for Henry Shapcott and gave very sound evidence about him. Miles Morgan and Henry Shapcott were lodgers at the house owned by Jonathan Hatton and on the morning of the 30th July Hatton stated '*I let Shepcot and Morgan into my house. Shepcot in his shirtsleeves, without his coat. I saw him the evening before he went out to go to the club and he did not take his coat but was in his shirtsleeves'*. Miles Morgan backed up this evidence by saying, '*Shepcot was dressed in cord trowsers, a check shirt I believe, a waistcoat, and no coat or jacket'*.

The magistrates deliberated for a while over the evidence in front of them and came to the conclusion that Mary McCarthy had correctly identified Henry Shapcott who was then committed for trial at the next Gloucester assizes and removed to Gloucester Prison. John Lea was discharged, as the case could not be positively proved against him. On the following Monday Hiram Archer was brought in front of the magistrates who stating that he seemed to have been 'the principal actor in the case' had no hesitation in committing him for trial at Gloucester along with the others.

1 GRO Q/Gli 16/1
2 Whiting. *Prison reform in Gloucestershire.* Appendix E (3)
3 *Ibid.* Chap. xvii Crime and punishment. Prisons and discipline.
4 Whiting. *Littledean House of Correction.* p. 31
5 GRO Q/SM 3/6 pp. 353-9
6 *Ibid.,* Q/Gli 3/4 6th December 1847
7 *Ibid.,* Q/Gli 16/5
8 *Ibid.*
9 *Ibid.,* Q/Gli 11/1 no.10
10 *Ibid.,* Q/Gli 12 no.11 June 1847
11 *Ibid.,* Q/Gli 4 19th June 1847
12 *Ibid.,* Q/Gli 17/5 1847
13 *Ibid.,* Q/Gli 22/1
14 *Ibid.,* Q/Gli 4 no. 13
15 *Ibid.,* Q/Gli 16/5
16 *Ibid.,* Q/Gli 20
17 *Ibid.,* Q/Gli 17/7
18 *Slaters Trade Directory.* 1852
19 *Monmouthshire Merlin.* 9th August 1851
20 GRO Q/Gli 13
21 *Ibid.,* Q/Gli 16/5/103
22 *Ibid.,* Q/Gli 10/4
23 *Monmouthshire Merlin.* 18th September 1851
24 *Ibid.*

Chapter Five

CONFINEMENT

T he Summer Assizes in 1851 started on the 9th August and were held at the Shire Hall in Gloucester in one of the two semicircular courtrooms at the rear of the building.[1] The Oxford circuit judge T. B. Martin swore in the jury and on Thursday the 14th August Richard Kear, James James, George Charles and Thomas Stephens were brought into court. Joining them was Thomas James who had been arrested for the same crime and brought straight to Gloucester for trial.

The indictment was first read as follows:

'The Jurors for our Lady the Queen upon their Oath present that <u>Richard Kear</u> late of the Township of West Dean in the County of Gloucester Labourer <u>James James</u> late of the same place Labourer <u>George Charles</u> late of the same place Labourer <u>Thomas Stephens</u> late of the same place Labourer and <u>Thomas James</u> late of the same place Labourer on the thirtieth day of July in the year of our Lord one thousand eight hundred and fifty one with force and arms at the Township aforesaid in the County aforesaid in and upon one Mary Macarthy in the peace of God and our said Lady the Queen then and there being, violently and feloniously did make an assault and that the said Richard Kear her the said Mary Macarthy then and there against her will violently and feloniously did ravish and carnally know And that the said James James, George Charles, Thomas Stephens, and Thomas James then and there feloniously were present aiding abetting and assisting the said Richard Kear the felony and rape aforesaid to do and commit against the form of the Statute in such case made and provided and against the peace of our said Lady the Queen her Crown and Dignity'.[2]

Four more counts followed in which each of the other accused were named as raping Mary McCarthy while the other defendants 'aided etc'. A sixth count simply named all five defendants together as raping Mary McCarthy.

Mary McCarthy was then brought into the courtroom and on oath repeated her story. She was cross-examined by Mr. Cooke who inferred that her credibility was doubtful and that her statement was unworthy of belief. '*His lordship interfered once or twice, and requested Cooke to ask the witness direct questions on the subject, if any asked at all as he felt it his duty to protect the witness. Cooke said he must question the witness as he had been instructed'*.[3] Mrs. Ann Jenkins gave evidence next and described the terrible condition that Mary was in that night and this was followed by a statement to the same effect by Constable William Ellis who had found Mary in the morning. Mr. Humble, the surgeon of the Westbury-on-Severn Union Workhouse, then described the injuries sustained by Mary and stated *'she has been under my care until within the last day or two'*.[4]

Constable Russell consulted his notebook and repeated what Stephens and Kear had said when arrested. Stephens said *'I saw an Irish woman at the cabin, I let her into the cabin but had nothing to do with her'*. Kear said he was innocent *'that he was at the club meeting at the Nag's Head, and went from thence to the Old Croft colliery, when he saw the woman; she complained she was very ill, and asked him if there was any water; that Hiram Archer went into the cabin with her and that he (Kear) should say no more about it'*. Stephens went on to say that *'he saw the woman about four o'clock, hearing her crying out'*. He walked down the road with her, and she complained of having been pulled about by some men.

A labourer named Hawkins, however, told a very different story. He said that he had been at the Nag's Head on the Tuesday night and went to the coke ovens where he fell asleep. In the morning he was woken by his friend Thomas Morgan who told him that he had seen Kear and Stephens in the morning a little before six and that Kear had said *'we had an Irish woman in the cabin'* and they wanted him (Morgan) to serve her as they had, but he would not. Mr. Cooke dismissed this evidence as being hearsay but of course the jury had heard it. This closed the case for the prosecution.

Mr. Cooke then addressed the jury on behalf of the prisoners. He begged them not to be influenced by what they had doubtless seen in the papers, which in these days of the 'march of improvement' were in the habit of heading such cases as this 'Horrible Outrage', or some such attractive title. They doubtless approached the case with great disgust, but he implored them to dismiss all they had read or heard from their minds, and confine their attention entirely to the evidence that had been adduced before them. The learned counsel proceeded to contend that the identity of the prisoners was not sufficiently established to convict them, and that the woman's testimony was not to be believed'.[5]

The judge summed up by reiterating the evidence against the prisoners, and the jury retired. When they returned they gave a unanimous verdict of guilty. His Lordship in passing sentence, remarked, with much feeling that the prisoners had been convicted of about the most abominable offence he had ever heard proved against a man. After briefly referring to the case, he went on to observe that he was glad for his own sake the old law had been altered; for though he believed no judge ever sat upon the bench more unwilling to carry out the extreme penalty of the law, had the old law still been in existence he should have considered it his duty to sentence four of the prisoners to death.[6] The amendment to the old law came into effect in June 1841 when punishment of death for the crime of rape was commuted to transportation 'beyond the

Seas' for the term of the prisoner's natural life. The judge continued his summing up by saying that he felt Thomas Stephens and Thomas James had shown some feeling towards the poor woman when she appealed to them for mercy and so their sentence was to be transportation for 15 years. His Lordship then sentenced Richard Kear, George Charles and James James to transportation for life for *'behaving most brutally'*.

The five men were then returned to Gloucester Prison where they were to spend the next few months. They must have been filled with horror at their sentence, as they now knew that they might never see their families and friends again. Richard Kear would have been desperately saddened that his little daughter Phoebe would grow up not knowing her father.

Gloucester Castle had originally housed the gaol and it was not until the eighteenth century that any prison reforms were carried out. In John Howard's book *The State of the Prisons* he gives a description of the county gaol, situated in what was left of Gloucester Castle as *'considerably in need of repair'*. He wrote of disease caused by lack of washing facilities and only one sewer, lack of segregation of the sexes resulting in a number of children being born within the prison and famine due to an inadequate diet. The county magistrates headed by Sir George Onesiphorus Paul introduced a number of rules to improve the situation in 1783 whilst agreeing to build a new prison. When the building work finally started in 1787 it was decided to keep the prisoners in part of the old gaol whilst the rest was demolished to obtain building materials.[7] To avoid overcrowding during this time the government decided to remove prisoners sentenced to transportation as quickly as possible. The prisoners were finally moved into the new prison in July 1791, with the only event to mar the first few months of this model prison being the escape of James Nichols on the 22nd October 1791 who used a ladder left lying around by workmen to get away.

The prison consisted of the gaol, which housed prisoners awaiting trial, debtors, those convicted of misdemeanours and those condemned to death. The penitentiary housed convicted felons, persons whose death sentence had been commuted and those awaiting transportation. The name penitentiary arose from the way that it was hoped that prisoners would spend the first third of their sentence reflecting on their criminality. After reflection behind bars, it was intended that prisoners should be gradually reintegrated into the society of other inmates, in preparation for their return to the outside world. Thirdly there was the house of correction for prisoners sentenced within the City of Gloucester at the petty sessions. The different classes of prisoners were to be kept separate, although all used the chapel and the infirmary.

Periodically rearrangements and additions were made to the cells but overcrowding was a real problem. By 1819 an account of Gloucester Prison showed that male prisoners were forced to sleep in rooms normally used as condemned cells, in cells set aside for female prisoners and even beds in the infirmary were used as sleeping quarters. The idea of just one prisoner to a

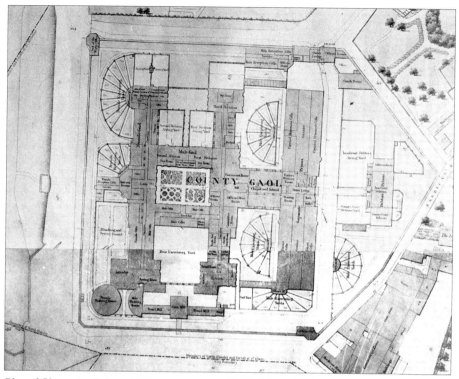

Plan of Gloucester Prison, 1852.   GRO Q/CR 27, Crown Copyright Reserved

room was non-existent and although the cells were swept daily and washed weekly the yards and workrooms were invariably in a filthy state.[8]

After the new model prison at Pentonville was completed by the end of 1842 the state of all prisons in Britain was studied with the result that all prison designs had to be approved by the surveyor-general of prisons, Joshua Jebb. He was one of the designers of Pentonville, and new rules about the design of prisons were so strict that it is not surprising that the wings of Gloucester Prison should strongly resemble Pentonville. A newspaper article in 1844 states that the alterations are about to be undertaken and Bond's *History of Gloucester* published in 1848 records that the prison *'had recently been considerably enlarged'*.

In the *Gloucester Journal* on the 19th October 1850, just a year before Richard Kear and the others went to Gloucester Prison, a very detailed article describes not only the condition of the prison buildings, but also how the prisoners lived and worked. A reporter for the newspaper accompanied the visiting justices when they toured the newly completed blocks and refurbished wings of the prison and the report gives a good idea of the conditions that the men from the Forest of Dean had to endure. With a few small omissions it is worth quoting the entire article:

'The County prison may be roughly described as consisting of three ranges of buildings, parallel to each other, and connected in the middle by two or three buildings at right angles with them. The magistrates passed into the main body of the prison, through a corridor, which divides the wings of the new prison, and opening into a spacious piazza, (if it may be so styled,) upon the columns of which stands the chapel. Two spiral iron staircases, climbing curiously upward, form a communication between the two floors. On the right and left are the airing grounds of the prisoners. These consist of four or five spaces, partially roofed and divided by walls, each of which, as well as the whole space, is shaped like a wedge, and opening into a common room at the small end; so that one officer stationed there can, through peep holes in the doors, overlook the whole of the prisoners' wards whilst they are taking exercise. The magistrates surveyed these parts of the building; the spacious apartment assigned to the visiting justices, and other minor accommodations, and then entered the separate prison.

The building consists of three tiers of cells, and they are at present occupied by different classes of prisoners. In one wing are the untried prisoners, and in the other those who have been convicted. In one tier are those employed in weaving, in another the shoemakers, and so on. The two upper tiers are surrounded by light iron galleries, reached by staircases also of iron, placed near the extremities of the wings. The corridor is lighted by windows sunk in the vaulted roof, and by a large window at each end. The cells are each lighted by panes of thick waved glass, which, added to the height of the window, prevent the prisoner from seeing beyond his cell. Peeps into the cells disclosed a somewhat curious scene - fellow creatures, cut off from society. One was busily weaving mats at a loom; another making shoes, surrounded by his tools; a third picking oakum with his fingers; whilst now and then he would drop his work, and gaze earnestly at the closed door, attracted by the unwonted sound of voices with which the building echoed.

The furniture of the cells consists of a table, a three-legged stool, and an open corner cupboard, clean and white as new wood; and on the top of the latter the prisoners hammock is placed in the day-time, made up not in nautical fashion, but like a roll of carpeting. A wash-hand basin, with water tap and waste pipe, a gas burner, and a copy of the prison regulations relative to the care and treatment of prisoners, are the remaining articles, which are noticeable. The supply of water is limited in quantity, but is sufficiently abundant for all necessary purposes; and the gaslight is extinguished at gunfire. The cells were pictures of cleanliness and order, whilst the few articles in use were turned to an ornamental purpose by their arrangement on the shelves of the cupboard. For instance, the tin pannikin, bright and shining, rested on a cushion formed by the fold of a clean towel, and was supported on one side by a knife and on the other side by a comb, just as tidy servant maids lay out their crockery on the kitchen shelf. A handle enables the inmate of the cell to strike a gong in the gallery and summon the turnkey, whilst in pulling the handle, a plate bearing the number of the cell, flies off from the outside wall, and shows the officer which prisoner it is who has given the signal. Some of the magistrates thought the ventilation of the cells was defective and complained of an offensive odour. However true this may have been, the cells are superior to the dwellings of large masses of the working classes. It is said, indeed, that people require increased comforts when they are shut up as criminals, to sustain their mental depression. The aspect of the corridor is stern, without being severe or cold. The fittings are complete, without anything superfluous. The light, falling on the black stone pavement of the corridor, is prison-like, without being either gloomy or gay. The staircases and galleries being of iron, and therefore light and airy, are an ornament to the building, like rigging to a ship. Finally, the place has a quiet look, and this is heightened when the silence is occasionally broken by the low sounds and hollow echoing of the footfall of the warders who march to and fro on duty.

The magistrates passed from the first floor gallery of the new prison into the chapel. This is a square apartment of considerable size, and cheerfully lighted by long circular headed windows. An open wood roof is the only appearance of ornament. A narrow gallery over the altar contains the pulpit on either side of which are slabs bearing the Ten Commandments. The seats in the body of the chapel are divided by an ingenious arrangement of the doors into 400 separate boxes, the occupants of which can all see the minister, but cannot see each other. This is effected by raising the seats row by row, like a steep gallery, so that each prisoner looks over the head of the prisoner before him, whilst in the very midst of the seats there is a sort of watch tower, from which a warder can survey the whole of the congregation. A large disc mounted on a pole, and exhibiting moveable figures, which stood on the floor, attracted attention by its singularity; it is a telegraph, by which the officers are enabled to move the prisoners between their cells and the chapel without uttering a single word.

The magistrates left the corridor by a door at its east end, and entered the victualling department, which forms part of the middle range of buildings. The attention was attracted, in the first place, by a steam engine, the two boilers embedded as usual, in brickwork, whilst the blackness of the iron and the brightness of the brass, showed that, after all, the engineer in charge of it wore a smutty jacket and had a smutty face, not because he is a sloven, but only because he could not help it. The cooking, washing, and warming of the gaol are done by steam. The spacious kitchen, which adjoins the engine room, contains a row of copper boilers, in one of which soup was being boiled by a jet of steam let in under and round it. Disjointed fragments of conversation were heard amidst a running commentary of hissing steam. The bread room next to the kitchen was then visited, and the prisoners' rations of bread and cheese pronounced good - 'very good' - by those who tasted them. Then the crowd streamed out in a long line, through a dark passage, penetrating to the centre of this range of the buildings, and at the end of it entered the penitentiary prison.

These buildings form three sides of a square, and the fourth opens towards the treadmill. The windows are filled with thick iron gratings, and the galleries bristle with spiked railings; yet the appearance of the place is agreeable rather than miserable. The grates may be regarded as trellis work, the balconies as pleasant little perches in the air, and then the prison loses its heavy look, and assumes the air of a pleasant old mansion, well secured to keep rogues out instead of in. The treadmill was the next object of attention, and was in motion. The prisoners were dressed in motley, one arm, one leg, and one half of the whole man being blue, and the other yellow. We can compare these gaolbirds to nothing more apt than goldfinches. Whilst some were clinging by their hands working on the wheel, others were collected in the yard, walking in a weary round to escape catching cold, and to stretch their legs. Every now and then as the wheel revolved, a whitened step appeared, and then one of the workers would drop down, and one of the walkers would get up, and so the wheel and the punishment was kept moving. Not a word was spoken on the wheel, or off it, nor was it necessary; for each prisoner knew the moment that his spell had ceased, so accurately, that he, whose turn had come, had no opportunity of forgetting it. One could not fail to be struck by the air of languor, and almost misery, which marks labour not lightened by reward'.

The sentence of penal servitude was divided roughly into three stages. For those sentenced to transportation this would have started with a first stage of nine months solitary confinement, with little or no talking allowed, except during the period allotted for exercise and prayers. During the second stage prisoners worked for three months under close supervision at employment on public works. The third stage, which lasted for the remainder of the sentence was transportation to public works in one of the colonies.

Richard Kear, George Charles, Thomas Stephens, James James and Thomas James were held under sentence of transportation in this separate confinement and for the next few months they would have to endure the unvarying monotony of the hard labour system of chapel – breakfast – treadwheel labour – dinner – treadwheel labour – supper – bed. Two treadwheels were used in Gloucester, one for grinding in the mill and the other for 'working unproductively'.[9] The new prison at Pentonville had introduced a change in the rules for separate confinement which were much more lenient. It was suggested that a schoolmaster introduce a regime of suitable employment in the prisoner's cell such as weaving, carpentry or sack making, together with instruction. However, in the County chairman's report for Gloucester Prison in 1850 he argues that '*I should exceedingly lament the superseding of the present system of Tread-Wheels, – as we should then be deprived of the employment of that wholesome system of coercion and monotonous Hard Labour, by which alone the sentences of the Court are carried out – which forms the most fitting punishment for the hardened convict, – and affords that salutary example through him to incipient offenders, to deter them from the further prosecution of a course of crime, which is the sole foundation of all legal penalties*'. During the 1850s the commissioners of prisons abandoned some features of the solitary regime at Gloucester such as the separate stalls in the chapel, the solitary exercise pens, and the horrific iron masks that prisoners wore in the corridors to prevent them from recognising each other, but the rule of no talking and the dreaded treadwheel was still very much the order of the day. The severity of their crime meant that men from the Forest of Dean would have been submitted to the harshest punishment going.

The Gloucester Prison registers give much the same physical description as at Littledean, only adding for Richard Kear that his face was pock marked, he had a blue mark on his forehead and nose and the bulge of his nose was very low.[10] The register also notes the religion of each of the men. Thomas James was given as 'any place of worship', Richard Kear gave his religion as 'Ranters' and the rest all said 'Church'.

On arrival the convicts were searched for any knives or other sharp instruments and an inventory was made of all their meagre possessions. Next they were stripped naked, examined by a doctor to make quite sure that they would be fit for hard labour, bathed and shaved. Their hair was closely cropped and they were clothed in the institutional uniform which consisted of '*a flannel waistcoat, calico shirt, worsted stockings and cotton handkerchief*'.[11] This distinct uniform, half in yellow and half in blue had the broad black arrows on it to show that it belonged to Her Majesty's prison. More often than not an indiscriminate bundle would be thrown at the prisoner as he stepped out of his bath and consequently most clothes had not the semblance of fitting. In the old Gloucester Prison inmates had to depend on their family for food, and, as a result these people had to be given free access to the prison yard. By 1850, prisoners were only allowed visits by next of kin every six months and no food, bedding or furniture was allowed in from the outside. Onesiphorous Paul argued, that in order to introduce method and order into a prisoner's life he needed to sever all links with the outside world. To do this Paul suggested that the county should provide a diet for all inmates.

The visiting justice's journal[12] gives details of the amended diet, which was introduced in July 1851 to all classes of prisoners. Richard and the others were Class 4 prisoners who were men employed at hard labour for terms exceeding six weeks but not more than four months; and convicted prisoners not employed at hard labour for terms exceeding four months. Breakfast for the Class 4 category prisoners would have been 8oz. of bread and 1 pint of gruel, lunch 8oz. of bread, 8oz. of potatoes and 3oz. of cooked meat without the bone and supper was the same meal as breakfast. This was clearly inadequate for the men as an entry in the visiting justice's minute book for November 1851 states '*one of the penitentiary prisoners complained of insufficiency of food*'. Another incident noted in the same minute book on the 13th December shows that the food was not entirely wholesome either, '*A complaint was made by William Dutton a prisoner in the penitentiary that there were grits and rats dung in his oatmeal gruel yesterday*'. The entry does, however, continue with a comment from one of the visiting justices '*I desired the stock of oatmeal to be examined and nothing of the kind was found*'.[13]

Henry Shapcott, who had been arrested some time after the others, arrived at Gloucester Prison on the 19th September to await trial at the next assizes.

His name had been spelt in many different ways throughout the various reports and registers but from the time he was received at Gloucester the form 'Shapcot' or 'Shapcott' was the most usual. The only addition to his description in the prison register was that he had 'two scars top of left arm'.[14] He was joined on the the 22nd September by Hiram Archer who had been pointed out by Mary McCarthy as the first man to commit the offence against her. His description only added that he had *'several moles, right and one on left side of neck and a scar on right shoulder blade'*.[15]

The pair of them were brought into court on the 2nd April 1852 in front of Judge Baron Platt and again Mary McCarthy and the other witnesses told their story. Both were found guilty and sentenced to transportation for life.

During the time that the men were confined to their cells they were provided with books, if they could read, and were daily visited by the Chaplain, *'and the*

No.	Name.	Offence for which Convicted.	Period for which Maintained. From. To. Inclusive.		Weeks.	Days.	£.	s.	d.
			Gloucester County Prison						
			A Return of the Amount paid during the half year ending the thirtieth day of September 1851 for Food. Clothing. Bedding and Fuel on Account of Prisoners kept at the expence of the County of Gloucester, who have been sentenced at the Assizes and Quarter Sessions shewing in such Return the Name of each Prisoner, the Offence for which he was Convicted the period during which he was maintained and the Amount paid per Week for such maintenance. —						
156	Richard Kear	Rape	"	"	7	4			
157	James James	The like	"	"	7	4			
158	George Charles	The like	"	"	7	4			
159	Charles Halliday	Manslaughter	"	"	7	4			
160	Thomas Stephens	Rape	"	"	7	4			
161	Thomas James	The like	"	"	7	4			

Gloucester Prison returns for the half year ending 30th September 1851.   GRO Q/CR 27

Schoolmaster, at such times as may be prescribed by the Chaplain'.[16] Convicted prisoners were allowed to send and receive one letter in the course of each quarter of the year and were able to receive visitors once every three months after the first three. Richard Kear may have seen his wife and daughter and other members of his family during his time at Gloucester but it is doubtful if he saw them again for many years. The Visiting Justice's Minute book for the 17th December 1851 states *'Governor absent with two officers, Wait and Cambridge with convicts to London'.*[17] Richard Kear, Thomas James, James James and George Charles were removed to Millbank prison on that day. Thomas Stephens was not well enough to go with them but a report from the medical officer to the Secretary of State on the 24th February 1852 stated that he was now fit for removal, and he joined the other men at Millbank on the 10th May 1852.

Henry Shapcott and Hiram Archer had to work through the first part of their solitary confinement at Gloucester Prison and in April 1852 the friends and family of Henry Shapcott raised a petition, which was carefully worded by Mr. W. James Knight Smith a solicitor of Newnham and sent to Mr. Poole a solicitor in London. It was forwarded to the Secretary of State for the Home Department and the letter accompanying the petition states *'We have the honour to enclose a Petition from the Township of West Dean in the County of Gloucester praying for a remittal of the sentence passed at the last Assizes on Henry Shapcott found guilty on, we believe, very insufficient evidence of a rape on Mary McCarthy,*

Under Sentence of Transportation in the County Prison.

	Names.	Ages.	Crimes Convicted of.	Dates of Conviction.	Terms of Transportation.
1	Jacob Harrison	44	Feloniously receiving stolen goods	Trinity Sessions, June 27, 1848	seven years
2	Jane Williams	42	Stealing a sheet	Epiphany Sessions, January 2, 1849	ditto
3	Thomas Woodham	77	Beastiality	Spring Assizes, March 29, 1849	life
4	John Careless	49	Stealing a post letter	.... ditto	seven years
5	John Spencer	19	Ditto lead	Epiphany Sessions, January 1, 1850	ditto
6	Thomas Hill	33	Rape on a child	Spring Assizes, March 30, 1850	fifteen ditto
7	Henry Webb	27	Stealing brass	Trinity Sessions, July 1, 1851	fourteen ditto
8	James Young	20	Ditto potatoes and a basket	.... ditto	ten ditto
9	William Cox	23	Ditto pigs	.... ditto	ditto
10	Thomas Gillman	23	Ditto lead	.... ditto	ditto
11	Edwin Tooth	25	Ditto umbrellas	.... ditto	ditto
12	Thomas Smith	23	Robbery, accompanied with wounding	Summer Assizes, August 9, 1851	life
13	James Brown	21	Ditto	.... ditto	ditto
14	Richard Kear	24	Rape	.... ditto	ditto
15	James James	28	Ditto	.... ditto	ditto
16	George Charles	22	Ditto	.... ditto	ditto
17	Charles Halliday	29	Manslaughter	.... ditto	ditto
18	Thomas Stephens	21	Rape	.... ditto	fifteen years
19	Thomas James	20	Ditto	.... ditto	ditto
20	James Adams	32	Forgery	.... ditto	ten ditto
21	Peter De Bar	26	Stealing lead	.... ditto	seven ditto
22	Thomas Bulver	22	Burglary	.... ditto	ditto
23	Joseph Hooper	28	Perjury	.... ditto	ditto

Calendar of Prisoners 14th October 1851.   GRO Q/SG *and request that you will be pleased to lay the same before Her Majesty for her gracious consideration'*.[18]

The petition itself began by giving details of the case and saying that *'when the sentence was pronounced Hiram Archer (who was on trial at the same time) said "My Lord I am sorry to say that I am guilty and deserve my punishment but this lad (meaning the said Henry Shapcott) is entirely innocent"'*.[19] Many of Henry Shapcott's friends were in court for both the petty sessions and assize court trials and they believed that Mary McCarthy had wrongly identified Henry as the eighth man to assault her. At the petty sessions Mary *'identified the said Henry Shapcott by his then and there being dressed in the same clothes and particularly in the same jacket as the one he wore at the time she stated he assaulted and ravished her'*.[20] By the time Henry Shapcott was brought to the assize court Mary identified him *'by his features, and by a small burn mark upon the left side of his neck, and she then and there stated she could not remember what dress he wore on the said 29th day of July last'*.[21]

All of Henry's friends had been with him at the Nag's Head on the night of the assault and in the petition they all swore, *'the said Henry Shapcott was then in his shirt sleeves, and without any jacket or coat'*. One of the petitioners, John Osborn, who had been at the assizes, stated that Mary McCarthy *'could only swear to one other person than the five, and that was Archer'*. Attached to the petition was a letter from Albert Jackson, who had been counsel for Henry Shapcott at his trial, endorsing the plea for clemency.

On the 5th July 1852 a report was sent to the Secretary of State by Mr. Baron Platt, the assize court judge who had originally convicted Henry Shapcott and Hiram Archer. The report, whilst agreeing with the statements made in the petition, set about proving that the conviction should stand. Mr. Platt started by explaining that the statement made by Hiram Archer who admitted his guilt at the trial and said that Shapcott was innocent *'may have been a manoeuvre, not unusual for offenders in the like desperate condition to adopt, in order to rescue an associate in iniquity; and cannot be trusted'*.[22] The fact that Mary McCarthy had been unsure as to the dress of Shapcott was explained by Platt as unimportant as Mary had definitely identified Shapcott as the 8th man to enter the cabin. Judge Platt continued by saying that although Hatton and Morgan had sworn that Henry Shapcott had not been wearing a jacket that night, he found that to be *'a sort of undress of very improbable selection for his attendance at a feast as one of the guests'*. This statement surely shows how far removed the Judge was from the hardworking miners of the Forest of Dean. The petition had argued that Henry Shapcott had remained at home after the event instead of running away as a guilty man would have done. The judge felt that this was only for greater security and to give him time to build up a plausible petition with his friends. The report ended with a comment that *'The jury, who throughout the assizes seemed to me to act with remarkable caution, were satisfied that the woman's story was true, and that she was not mistaken in pointing out Shapcott as the 8th of the men who*

Gloucester County Assize.   PRO ASSI 5/172/4

violated her person,' and Judge Platt concluded by saying *'I think they were right; and that the petition on behalf of Shapcott is an attempt to defeat justice'.*

Henry Shapcott and Hiram Archer were received at Millbank Prison on the 7th September 1852. This was to be the last time that the seven men would all be in the same prison.

1   *VCH* (Glos. city vol.) p. 249
2   PRO ASSI 5/171
3   *Gloucester Journal* 14th August 1851
4   *Ibid.*
5   *Ibid.*
6   *Ibid.*
7   Whiting. *Prison reform in Gloucestershire 1776-1820.* p. 14
8   *Ibid.*
9   Regulations for the government of the County prison at Gloucester 1844 (GRO PS11)
10 GRO Q/Gc 6/2
11 *Ibid.,* as at 9.
12 Visiting justices journal Q/Gc 1/6 1851
13 *Ibid.*
14 GRO Q/Gc 6/2
15 *Ibid.*
16 *Ibid.,* as 9.
17 *Ibid.,* as 12.
18 PRO HO 18/333
19 *Ibid.*
20 *Ibid.*
21 *Ibid.*
22 *Ibid.*

Chapter Six

MOVING ON

L ines of manacled prisoners were a common sight as they were moved from prison to prison. They were most regularly to be seen at railway stations where there was always a crowd to jeer and point in disgust. Richard Kears' wife Charlotte may have been at Gloucester station on the morning of the 17th December 1851, and friends and families of all the men would have found it difficult to hold back the tears as they said their farewells. The prisoners had a last glimpse of familiar surroundings and faces, as with a shriek from the engine the train pulled slowly out of the station.

Richard Kear, Thomas James, James James and George Charles were together in the carriage and at least the officers who were in charge of them allowed the men to talk and chatter, as they liked. Even though the handcuffs grated harshly at first the men soon became philosophical about the future they were now facing. For a short while the strict discipline and regime of

Gloucester station 1852 from Measom's Illustrated Guide to the Great Western Railway.
Courtesy Gloucester Library

Waggon passing Millbank Penitentiary. An engraving from a drawing by T. H. Shepherd taken from J. Elmes' Metropolitan Improvements; or London in the Nineteenth Century *published in 1828.*   British Library

silence of the last few months in Gloucester Prison was forgotten as the four men recalled their lives in the Forest of Dean and comforted themselves. They would have spoken about the sentences they had received and although they may have heard of people being transported to foreign shores they probably presumed that they would be sent to Australia.

When the train made one of its scheduled stops prisoners could be seen begging for tobacco from people on the platform. *'Several people threw tobacco in at the windows of our carriage, which officers in vain tried to prevent, but what they did was but for show, and to keep up the appearance of doing their duty'.*[1] As the train approached London the men would have craned their necks to see the unfamiliar sights. Vauxhall Gardens with its huge theatrical looking summer house, half tumbling to decay; the gasworks with tall chimneys and a glimpse of the Lambeth potteries with earthen pans and tubing arranged along the walls. They stopped on the viaduct over Westminster Bridge Road whilst tickets were collected, and from there they could see the dreary-looking attics of houses, cabs and carts and above all, crowds of people.

The noise and hustle and bustle of Paddington railway station would have been both bewildering and exciting for the men as they were pushed through the crowds to the waiting horse drawn black maria for the short journey to Millbank Penitentiary. The small dark compartment of the long hearse-like van had a number of doors on each side through which the prisoners were pushed one by one. They found themselves in a small box which was none too clean and not too well ventilated. The sides had narrow gratings out of which they vainly tried to glimpse the new world they were entering. These prison buses were built to accommodate about twenty prisoners but upwards of thirty were usually conveyed[2] and it is certain that Richard and his friends now met other convicts all bound for the same destination.

Millbank had been built between 1812 and 1816 at a time when the deterrent value of transportation and short-term imprisonment in county gaols was becoming increasingly dubious. It was decided that a national penitentiary would provide long-term imprisonment giving a severe punishment of hard labour, solitude and a meagre diet. The construction of Millbank cost the enormous sum of £450,000, which the committee insisted

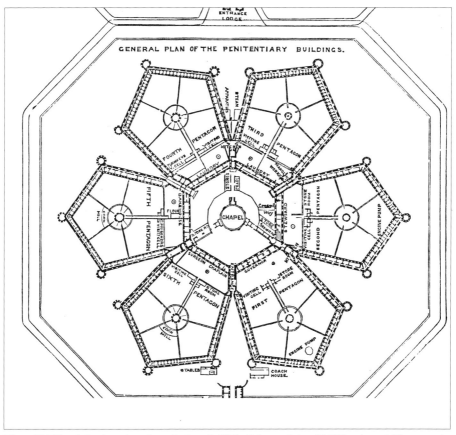

Plan of Millbank Penitentiary from Arthur Griffiths' Memorials of Millbank and Chapters in Prison History, *Vol. III, 1875.*

was caused by unforeseen difficulties in sinking foundations into the soggy bank of the river Thames.[3] The building was made up of seven pentagons which contained the cells, surrounding a central area housing the chapel. When it opened in 1817 it was the largest prison in Europe, capable of holding up to twelve hundred prisoners, and the immense yellow-brown mass of brickwork was described as 'a monument of ugliness'. It was such a maze of corridors that an old warder who had difficulty in finding his way around used to leave chalk marks on the walls to enable him to find his way back to the guardhouse.[4]

To start with the regime at Millbank was very strict with silence and hard labour enforced and a poor diet. Prisoners who had been used to easier times in county prisons soon rebelled and in 1818 riots broke out over the amount of bread they were given and soon after this the governor was fired. New rules were introduced limiting visits to ten minutes, taking away all reading material, and reducing the diet. In 1823 the prisoners were surviving on bread, gruel and watery soup, which caused a severe outbreak of typhus, dysentery and scurvy during which thirty-one died. The prison was closed temporarily with prisoners being sent to alternative accommodation. When Millbank re-opened in 1824 the regime was relaxed a little providing shortened sentences and an improved diet, which now included cocoa for breakfast and a broth made of beef and vegetables for dinner. The silent system was still enforced, but not very perfectly, and the routine of the day was only broken by chapel and exercise, with a weekly visit from one of the scripture readers or the chaplain. In 1850 there were *'1100 male prisoners confined at Millbank, 700 in separate cells; the remaining 400, after a period of about six months' separation are lodged in large dormitories, and take their meals and sleep under strict inspection day and night'*.[5]

It was dark by the time the van reached the forbidding outer lodge of Millbank Prison and as the heavy doors closed behind them the men were ushered into the reception room. As in Gloucester Prison they were once again searched for anything they might have acquired on the journey, even handkerchiefs were taken away. Their own clothes, which had been returned to them before they left Gloucester, were now thrown to one side and replaced by yet another prison dress. Even though it was winter it was not unusual for underclothing to be non-existent leaving the prisoners wearing rough jackets and trousers of indiscriminate colours, a vest, stockings and a worsted cap. All over the clothing were huge black arrows and even the heavy boots had the nails hammered in an arrow shape *'so that whatever ground you trod you left traces that Government property had travelled over it'*.[6]

Before putting on the prison uniform, the convicts were told to strip and take the usual bath. The baths in Millbank were similar to those in prisons all over the country. Walls of corrugated iron separated them and the depth of each bath was about 20 inches. The lower part of the bath was often coated

Prisoners waiting to be weighed at a medical inspection at Millbank in the 1880s.
courtesy of the Guildhall Library, Corporation of London

with cement and the line of grease, which built up through constant use, made the prisoners shudder as they got in. It was certainly '*not a very pleasant thing for a man to have to bathe in the same water along with men suffering from every variety of skin disease and cutaneous eruption*'.[7]

Finally after the customary medical examination and haircut the prisoners were issued with a number thus removing the last traces of their former self. Richard Kear was given no. 22542, James James no. 22543, George Charles no. 22544 and Thomas James no. 22537. These numbers were marked on an iron plate attached to the right breast pocket of the jacket and the number of the cell was marked in black on their backs. Whilst in Millbank, Richard Kear was put into six different cells and the others had two cells each.[8] During their stay at Millbank their conduct was given as 'good'. Thomas Stephens who had been unwell at Gloucester Prison arrived at Millbank later than the others in May 1852 and he was registered as no. 23313.[9] His behaviour during his stay was given as 'indifferent'. Henry Shapcott and Hiram Archer were sent to Millbank a few months later in September and were registered as nos. 23888 and 23889.[10]

From the reception area, all the prisoners were '*marched off down a passage and through a door at the foot of a winding spiral stone staircase in to the Pentagon yard – across this and through a gate or two in the dividing railings and into a similar door – up a spiral stone staircase like the first one – one flight – two flights – three flights – to the very top where they were transferred by the warder who had conducted them so far to another warder, and he at once pointed out the way along the passage to a cell, the door of which he opened'.*[11]

The cells at Millbank were lit by *'a small gas-jet protruding from the wall about 4 feet from the ground'*[12] and it was by this light that Richard Kear looked round his new home. A hammock was slung across one corner containing coarse linen sheets, a couple of blankets and a hair pillow. These hammocks had a division in the centre and as one prisoner wrote to his brother in the 1850s, *'they do not appear to be intended to sleep in so much as to exercise your powers as an acrobat, but with care you may get into them and sleep in one of their two divisions'.*[13] The list of other items in a typical cell at Millbank consisted of a *'wooden platter and spoon, a wooden saltbox, two tin pint mugs, a bright pewter chamber utensil, an ordinary school slate, a large wooden bucket or pail with wooden flat hoops and fitted with a close fitting lid, and a short-handled hair-broom or brush'.*[14] There was also a coarse towel hanging on a nail and a small piece of soap.

As the light of morning dawned Richard would have been woken by the prison bell at around 6 am. The warder unlocked the door of the cells and the prisoners were marched along the corridor to empty the slop-buckets and fill their water-cans. If they had time they could have a quick wash at a large stone trough and then it was back to the cell for the cleaning ritual. There was the floor to be scrubbed and all the utensils for washing in, or eating off had to be cleaned and polished. In many prisons the rules were rigidly enforced about this process and consequently some prisoners never used water from the tin jugs for fear of staining them. *'The result being that if the poor devil washed and kept himself clean he would be reported and severely punished for having dirty tin ware'.*[15] The other task to perform first thing in the morning was to fold up the hammock and bedclothes. This too, had to conform to prison rules, with the sheets on the inside, the blankets next and all to be rolled tightly in the hammock. While all this was happening breakfast would be served in the prisoners' cell, which was often still dark in the winter adding to the hardship of the daily chores.

At various times during the day all the prisoners were made to take exercise. Here too, silence was enforced which only added to the dejection that the men were feeling. Richard and his friends may have managed the odd word to each other as they circled the yard or they may have perfected a sort of deaf and dumb language learnt from fellow inmates, but the warders knew all the tricks. Friends were placed in separate circles within the exercise yard and in some prisons as soon as one man was released into the yard another was removed from the circling group to return to his cell, in this way ensuring that friends might never see each other.

Chapel was a very important part of the daily routine at Millbank, and one of the few times when the prisoners could use their voices. At these services early in the morning Richard Kear may have briefly remembered the lusty singing at the meetings in Oldcroft. The prison chaplain had a mission to educate the ignorant and to bring the wicked to repentance, which was a crucial part of Victorian prison reformation. The chaplain carried out his duties in several ways, by providing a sermon at the morning service, leaving religious tracts in the cells and visiting the prisoners personally. The sermon would have contained the usual words about the sins of the flesh, dishonesty, and over-indulgence in alcohol. The Rev. J. Penny was the chaplain in 1850 and was quite pleased when he was able to reduce his workload by appointing Mr. Postance as a scripture reader. Rev. Penny noted that '*Mr. Postance, the individual filling the office, having in cheerful compliance with the directions of the Chaplain, been in constant practice of visiting the cells for the purpose of reading the Word of God with the prisoners individually*'.[16]

Prison chaplains were also put in charge of assistant schoolmasters whose job was to test the capabilities of the prisoners and provide instruction for the less able. Once again prisoners used these assemblies for illicit conversation with fellow inmates, '*under the pretence of mumbling their lessons aloud they engaged in ribald chat, and many were making disgusting and licentious drawings on their slates and showing them to their pals*'.[17] Many men, however, who had never been able to read or write benefited from this schooling and those like Richard Kear who had received rudimentary instruction were able to extend their knowledge by reading from the many books in the prison library. Quite often the prisoner would have no choice over his reading matter. If he wished to change his book he was obliged to put it outside the cell door before he set about his work and the schoolmaster would deposit a replacement there in return. If the man had been in prison for some time he could, therefore, find himself reading the same book many times.

Although well meaning, the chaplains and the schoolmasters had to contend with extremely rough and unruly prisoners and whether they totally achieved the reformation, which was intended, is doubtful. However, the daily chapel service and the hour of schooling, perhaps once a week, did at least break the dreadful monotony of prison life. Rev. Penny wrote in his report of 1850 that '*it is satisfactory to state that instances of resolved carelessness or turbulence have been of rare occurrence*'.[18]

Of course, the main part of the day for the prisoners at Millbank, as in all prisons, was taken up with working. Although there was a treadwheel at Millbank, this form of punishment unlike Gloucester Prison, was usually reserved for the prisoner serving a shorter sentence. The men from the Forest of Dean still had six months or so to finish their first period of penal servitude which kept them in solitary confinement. Occupations for this class of prisoner were necessarily confined to those that could be carried out in a cell such as picking oakum, mat making or sewing. Oakum was the fibre from short lengths of old ships' rope, which had been picked apart. It was then re-spun into ropes, used as stuffing for mattresses, or it was sent to boatbuilders for sealing or caulking wooden ships. Most of the rope given to the prisoners would be extremely dirty and covered with tar and they were expected to pick at least three pounds a day. The men would often try and hide a nail in their cell which would help with the chore as failure to pick the required amount could mean a bread and water diet for several days. Alternative work for the prisoners in their cells was making coal sacks and mailbags. They were given pieces of very hard canvas and a large, often blunt needle to carry out this task, but most men preferred this punishment to the tedium of the oakum picking. The clothing for almost all the public works prisons was cut and made at Millbank and a register for 1854 shows that during a nine-month period, some 24,145 military greatcoats, 3,275 jackets and 3,442 pairs of trousers were produced.[19]

During the time that Richard and his friends were in Millbank they would have been allowed to send letters to their families. These were heavily censored by the chaplain, as were any letters that the prisoners received. As most of the inhabitants of the Forest of Dean were illiterate at that time it is doubtful if the families could ever read any letters that were sent to them or indeed if they ever replied. Prisoners were allowed to have visits from friends and family once every six months but again it would have been highly unlikely that anyone from Gloucestershire could have afforded the time or the money to come to London.

As a reward for industry and good conduct a small payment was paid to prisoners and as the records show that Richard Kear, George Charles, Thomas James and James James all had 'good' conduct whilst at Millbank they may well have received the 3d. a week which was the gratuity in 1852 for second class prisoners.[20] This amount was placed to a prisoners credit and transmitted to the Governor of the colony to which the prisoner was removed. On his release the money would be advanced to the prisoner, usually in small amounts, to stop it all being spent immediately in the nearest hostelry.

As vacancies occurred at Portland Prison and other establishments for public works, prisoners who had served their first period of solitary confinement of nine to twelve months were removed from Millbank. On the 25th August 1852 four of the men from the Forest of Dean were sent to Portland where they were registered with the following numbers:-Thomas James 2849 Richard Kear 2853, James James 2854 and George Charles 2855.[21] The greater sense of freedom which they encountered would have lifted their spirits and the fresh sea air renewed their tired bodies. They were set to work in the quarries cutting stone, which was used for the construction

Work being done on the Portland breakwater from an image in the Illustrated London News, *17th July 1852.* courtesy Gloucester Library

of a new breakwater. This was familiar work to the miners and as their bodies regained strength they may have accepted this form of imprisonment with a degree of willingness and cheerfulness, which they had not felt for a long time.

Portland Prison was opened in 1848 and there were two main reasons for its establishment. Firstly by employing convicts it provided cheap labour for the construction of the new breakwater. Secondly, the Prison Commissioners used it as a new system for dealing with prisoners who had been sentenced to transportation. Now, instead of being immediately sent to the colonies, prisoners who had spent one year in a closed prison like Millbank would spend a period on public works such as the Portland Breakwater. If they worked well and had good behaviour they could earn a 'ticket-of-leave,' which would entitle them to a considerable amount of freedom after transportation. *'All penal-servitude prisoners were subject after release to the conditions of what was known as "ticket-of-leave". The ticket of leave originated in Australian practice, permitting long-sentence men to complete their sentences working as labourers outside prison, but subject to recall if they should break the terms of their conditional release'.*[22] As most of the convicts who were sent to Australia had no prospect of ever returning home the 'ticket-of-leave' system was extremely beneficial in helping a man find employment as a start to a new life in the colonies.

By 1850 the system seemed to be working well and in his report of that year the surveyor general of prisons Lieut.Col. Jebb commented on a report from the Governor of Portland, Captain Whitty. Jebb said *'The subdued, improved, and disciplined state in which the convicts generally arrive at Portland, from the stage of separate confinement, appears to be an admirable preparative for their transfer to the greater degree of freedom unavoidable on public works. They are remarkably alive and submissive to treatment guided by good faith and impartiality, and with good officers to administer the system with firmness and humanity I see no reason whatever to doubt of its successful result'.*

Although the men responded well to this new prison regime, they were still locked up every night in small corrugated iron cells about 7ft. by 4ft. and 7ft. high. The main building of the prison consisted of four large open halls, a chapel, which could house 1,000 prisoners, an infirmary for 60, a bakery and accommodation for 24 unmarried warders. All this was enclosed within a high boundary wall. In August 1852 when the men from the Forest of Dean arrived, 402 convicts were employed on quarrying an average of 1220 tons of stone a day[23] for the breakwater. The remainder of the 800 or so inmates at that time were employed as general labourers, filling and shifting wagons, forming roads, and squaring stone, with a few put to work in the carpenters and blacksmiths shops.

The familiar routine of chapel and schooling continued at Portland and the chaplain, the Rev. J. Moran, gave details of the education provided in 1850. *'The whole number of prisoners is divided into twelve classes, each class consisting of seventy men. These classes are again sub-divided into two divisions, each of which one master superintends. Each whole class is opened by singing a hymn of two verses, after which a collect is repeated by one of the masters, and then a chapter of the Bible is read verse by verse by the prisoners. This occupies about fifteen or twenty minutes after which follows three hours of writing, reading, questions on arithmetic and the issuing of library books. The whole concludes with singing a verse and a blessing'.*[24]

'As regards the diet of convicts employed upon public works, it being an object that they should be made to exert themselves to the utmost, it has been found essential to give them such a diet as would support their strength'.[25] Lieut. Col Jebb's report went on to show that the men received more sugar, bread and meat than they had at Millbank. Scurvy was still a problem in most prisons and Portland was no exception. It was decided to introduce more vegetables into the diet to counteract this complaint but when the prisoners were presented with onions and lettuces they threw them out of their cells and this new idea was abandoned. The rule of silence was still enforced at Portland and even the exchange of a smile to a neighbour would be punished by a bread and water diet.

At Portland the convicts would often conceal pieces of stone or rusty nails, which they *'flung with terrific force from a pocket-handkerchief at the poor governor's head'.*[26] To avoid this happening, weekly cell searching was carried out by the warders. If they took a particular dislike to a prisoner the warders would wait until the men were at work and untidy the cells, unrolling bedding and throwing other items all over the floor. Along with the cell inspection was the daily body search which was imposed on the convicts. The warder would pass his hands very roughly down the body and the legs of the prisoner who would have to stand quite still and endure it. This process was a little resented by the prisoners but not nearly as much as the once monthly 'dry bath process'. This was a disgusting business starting

Prisoners working in a quarry on the Isle of Portland.   author's collection

with the prisoner being told to remove his clothes. The naked man was then asked to open his legs wide and stretch his arms above his head. His mouth was checked and then he was told to bend down and touch his feet with his fingers. The feeling of being touched by unfriendly hands was unbearable and yet they were compelled to submit to this degradation.

Every day groups of convicts were marched to the quarries, which were situated outside the prison walls. When the stone was dug it was loaded into railway trucks, which carried the load from the base of the inclines to the end of the staging where the stone was deposited. Escapes were often attempted by members of these working parties but with little success, however, just before Richard and his friends came to Portland, two men escaped by climbing through a drain. This resulted in a sentry post being set up on the road leading out of Portland and soldiers were stationed there during the prisoners' working hours.

Prisoners could not help but be aware of the enormous interest which the breakwater works held for the general public. Tourists were allowed right to the end of a railed walkway and in July 1852, just one month before the group of men from Gloucestershire arrived, Queen Victoria, her consort Prince Albert and their sons landed at Portland to inspect the progress. It was in these surroundings that the four men waited for transportation.

Thomas Stephens who had been unwell at Gloucester and Millbank was not fit enough for heavy work and was therefore not sent to Portland with the others. On the 22nd October 1852 he was sent to Dartmoor Prison where he was registered with the number 1577.[27]

Whilst Richard Kear, George Charles, Thomas James and James James were being held at Portland, Henry Shapcott and Hiram Archer were still in Millbank Prison. Very soon all six of them were to meet up again as they embarked on the biggest adventure of their lives.

[1]   Priestley. *Victorian Prison Lives*. p.219
[2]   *Ibid.*, p. 9
[3]   Ignatieff. *A Just Measure of Pain*. p.171
[4]   *Ibid.*, p. 171
[5]   Jebb. *Report on the Discipline and Management of the Convict Prisons, 1850*. p. 8.
[6]   See 1. above p. 22
[7]   *Ibid.*, p. 19
[8]   PRO PCOM 2/32 Prison Records - Millbank
[9]   PRO PCOM 2/33 Prison Records - Millbank
[10]   *Ibid.*
[11]   See 1. above p. 24
[12]   *Ibid.*, p. 29
[13]   Letter from a convict in Australia to his brother in England (*Cornhill Magazine* No.13, 1866)
[14]   See 1. above p. 32
[15]   See 1. above p. 83
[16]   See 5. above p. 9
[17]   See 1. above p. 110
[18]   See 5. above p. 9
[19]   Mayhew & Binny. *The Criminal Prisons of London*. p. 253
[20]   See 5. above p. 67
[21]   PRO PCOM 2/384
[22]   See 1. above p. 284
[23]   See 5. above
[24]   Bettey. *The Island and Royal Manor of Portland*. p. 125
[25]   See 5. above
[26]   Dent. *Two Commissions*. p. 33
[27]   PRO HO18/352/25

Chapter Seven

THE VOYAGE OF THE *EDWARD*

Thirty two convicts were put aboard the *Edward* at Portland on the 27th December 1852.[1] These men were the lucky ones, who by showing good conduct whilst in prison and retaining reasonable health and strength had been chosen to go to Bermuda instead of Australia. Convicts who were sent to Australia seldom returned, often preferring to find employment and a new life in this far off country once they received their ticket-of-leave. There was no provision for released prisoners on the small islands of Bermuda and they were returned to England at the end of their sentence, but the men from the Forest of Dean did not know this as the line began to move up the gangplank.

Richard looked across at his friends but they did not return his gaze, their heads hung low and he could see that the spirit had gone out of their bodies. They felt the pull on the shackles as the line began to move forward, Richard shut his eyes following blindly and wondering if he would ever see England or his home again.

Once on board the *Edward* the four men, Richard Kear, George Charles, Thomas James and James James were looped together in batches with a chain, which was run through their leg-irons and fastened to the deck. They stood, huddled together shivering in the cold sea air whilst trying to accustom themselves to the heaving of the deck beneath them.

The *Edward* had already embarked convicts being held at Woolwich before arriving at Portland. This batch of prisoners contained 11 men from the prison hulk *Warrior*, 30 from the *Defence* hulk, 41 men from Pentonville Prison and 25 from Wakefield Prison.[2] Among the 55 men which the *Edward* collected from Millbank Prison, Richard would have spotted Henry Shapcott and Hiram Archer. These two had been put on board on the 22nd November but because of the stormy weather they were forced to stay at anchor for several days before moving on to Portsmouth where they picked up another 22 men and then on to Portland. William Rogers the surgeon wrote in his journal about the delay, *'during our stay in England even had the weather permitted, it would not have been safe to have allowed many of the prisoners on deck at a time, for it is quite possible that some of them might have effected their escape'.*[3] Now all the men convicted in the Forest of Dean, with the exception of Thomas Stephens, were together again.

It was compulsory for all prisoners sent on board to have a medical certificate and any found to be unfit were put ashore. A further 30 convicts were put on board at Plymouth and at this stage, one man was discharged to Dartmoor as being unfit for the voyage. There were now 245 men on board and after a final check of their papers, the *Edward* finally left England on the 23rd January 1853.

Originally, ships used to transport convicts were merchantmen chartered into service to carry prisoners. A large number of them were Indian built ships very sturdily constructed, quite often of teak, which made them more seaworthy than the British vessels. Most were built at Calcutta and used for many years to carry cargoes around the ports of India and China before being used as convict ships. They were all square-rigged ships or barques, between 200 to 600 tons. Shipowners did have larger vessels but these could be used more profitably elsewhere and so they only tendered their smaller ships. Many of these transport ships had to endure dangerous voyages to Australia and unless shipowners could find a return cargo they became severely out of pocket, consequently the vessels usually alternated between carrying convicts or cargo or even fare paying passengers or immigrants.

The *Edward* was not built in India, but in Quebec, Canada in 1849 by Oliver for the owners, Restarick. Just before her maiden voyage to Bombay, she was brought to London to be registered and classed by Lloyd's. The survey was carried out both afloat and in Limekiln dry dock between October and December 1849, and the report gives great detail about her construction.[4] She is described as a sailing barque belonging to the port of Plymouth and her master at that time was named as Alexander Robertson. Her length was just over 130ft., breadth 27ft. and depth of hold 20ft. and her overall net tonnage was given as 590. She was mainly constructed of Quebec oak and hackmatack[5] with the decking of yellow pine and Quebec elm. The general quality of workmanship was given as 'good'. She had two fore sails, two fore topsails, two fore topmast staysails, two main sails and two main topsails all 'well found'.

The survey goes on to give details of the cables and anchors, which were stated to be 'all of good quality', as were the windlass, capstan and rudder. She had a long boat and two quarter boats. Under the heading 'General Remarks' it shows the examination carried out to the *Edward* necessary for the purpose of classing the ship. These included checking that all the iron and copper bolts were 'well-bolted thro and clinch' and 'air courses left open to examine timbers'. 'Treenails driven out at various parts for examination' were said to be ' sufficient' and it noted, 'the bottom caulked and sheathed with yellow metal'. The master, Mr. Robertson, and Mr. Middleton of Lloyd's both signed the document and the vessel was classed as A1 for five years from 1849.

In 1852 Lloyd's Register shows that the *Edward* was brought in for repairs to her hull. Her destination at that time was given as 'W.Inds.'. Lloyd's List for the 24th January 1853, column 5, has an entry for a vessel named *Edward* sailing from Plymouth on the 23rd January bound for Bermuda. The journey was to

Survey of the barque Edward, *1849.*   National Maritime Museum

take her just over a month, arriving on the 28th February 1853. By April 1853 she was back in Plymouth to take the next batch of convicts to Bermuda.

The day after the *Edward* set sail on the 23rd January she encountered very severe weather causing the vessel to pitch and roll heavily. The surgeon noted, *'nearly all of the prisoners were seasick, and they continued so, more or less, for upwards of a week, and on again meeting with strong winds, they again suffered quite as much from the sickness'*. In 1836 the government had decided not to send convicts out during the cold winter months but the gaols and prison hulks were becoming so overcrowded with men awaiting transportation that the well being of convicts on the voyage became a secondary consideration. All that mattered was the need to make room for the never-ending stream of new prisoners.[6] Wet through and extremely cold and ill, many of the convicts must have felt that this was punishment indeed.

All prisoners were washed thoroughly and given new clothing before being taken on board ship to try and minimise disease spreading. The clothes were generally of poor quality and although suitable for a summer voyage were altogether too light for a winter journey. Surgeons often had to cut up sheets and blankets to provide extra clothing as strong gales, high seas and heavy rain made the drying of clothes a long process.[7] Once on board the men from the Forest of Dean were taken to their quarters and issued with their bedding and eating utensils. They were all given a number and divided into groups of five or six. Each bunch of convicts was then pushed into a berth of approximately six feet square giving about 18 inches of space to sleep in. These berths were always dark with the only light filtering in through heavily grated hatches. The air was foul and because of the water that seeped in through the ship's seams the bedding was always damp and dank. Certainly during the first part of the voyage of the *Edward* with the ship tossing heavily it would have been quite common for the prisoners to be washed from their hammocks by a torrent of water.

The guards on board these transport ships were soldiers, either raw recruits or veterans who were often unruly and in poor health. They were often drunk and had to be severely disciplined whilst on board making their plight almost as unbearable as the prisoners. Guards were also needed to look after the prisoners on arrival in Bermuda. These men were non-commissioned officers whose wives and children sometimes accompanied them on the voyage, as the men could be stationed out there for several years. These families had to experience all the harsh conditions of the voyage, often requiring medical attention, but at least they had accommodation on dry land when they arrived.

The master of the *Edward* in 1853 was J. Adamson who on his trips to Bermuda may have referred to navigational notes issued by the Governor of Bermuda in 1846, particularly the section stating *'On leaving England for Bermuda, instead of steering a direct course for the destined port, or following the usual practice of seeking for the trade-winds, it may be found a better course, on the setting of an easterly wind, to steer West, and if this wind should veer by the South towards the West, to continue on the port-tack until, by changing, the ship could lie in its course … The quickest voyage from England to Bermuda, therefore, may perhaps be made by sailing on a course composed of many curved lines, which cannot be previously laid down, but which must be determined by the winds met with on the voyage'.*[8]

The next most important person was the Surgeon-Superintendent William Rogers. The naval surgeons selected by the Admiralty to become surgeon-superintendents had a much greater degree of responsibility by the 19th century, not only as a Royal Navy surgeon, but also as superintendent of the prisoners. His first job once on board was to check each convict to make sure that he was healthy enough for the voyage. He was also responsible for the cleanliness of the convicts and the cleaning and airing of their quarters. William Rogers appears to have been fairly considerate to the prisoners, as his journal shows, *'everything that could be done to ensure their comfort and health was carried out. The cleanliness of their persons, the dryness of the deck and thorough ventilation were the chief objects of consideration'.*[9] It was, after all, most important that healthy men were delivered to the convict establishments for the hard work in store for them, and besides, William Rogers knew that he would be paid for each prisoner disembarked in good health.

The surgeon-superintendent inspected each convict daily ensuring that every man received an ounce of lemon juice and sugar to guard against scurvy. He was expected to check that food for the prisoners was correctly cooked and served at the proper meal times. All the provisions and every cask of food had to be opened in his presence on deck to ensure that there was no pilfering by the guards. Generally the rations were of a good quality and those on board received a diet of preserved meat and potatoes supplemented by gruel every morning with sugar or butter in it, as well as bread or ships biscuit, rice and raisins. The provision of drinking water was a constant problem especially as most casks were filled from the Thames before embarkation. This water often went bad after a very short time and so, to supplement this, wine was issued as part of the weekly allowance.[10] One of the main problems which Rogers had to contend with in his role as medical officer, was seasickness which took its toll of many of the prisoners. Even after recovering from it several were left in a very weak state and another entry in the journal shows how sterilised milk was given to the sick '*as also to two of the wives and a child of the non commissioned officers of the guard. It was very much relished and is a most grateful beverage*'.

William Rogers was obviously a fairly accomplished medical officer as his journal gives great detail of the 'adhesion of the gall bladder' which caused the

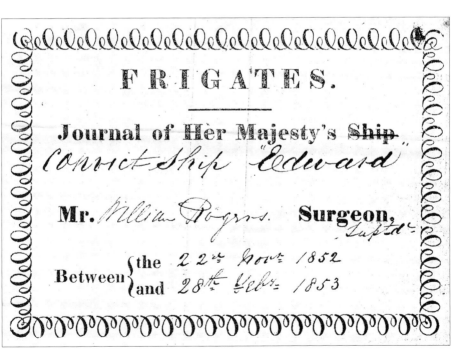

A portion of the front cover of the journal for Her Majesty's Convict Ship, Edward.
Public Records Office ADM 101

eventual death of John Lloyd on the voyage to Bermuda. He writes, *'had a favourable opportunity occurred of making microscopic examination of the diseased organs I should have much liked'*. This was the only death on the voyage of the *Edward* and, apart from the general debility of most of the prisoners due to seasickness, the only other man who was worthy of note was *'the person who was the subject of mania'*. Rogers continued this entry by saying that this man *'it would appear has been in an asylum previous to his conviction. He was very quiet unless irritated; his health has always been good. I understand he is to be sent home'*.

The daily routine on board the *Edward* was similar to that on all the transport ships, starting early around 5 am with the convicts chosen as cooks for the voyage being given the food to cook for breakfast. As the sun came up the convicts were all ushered onto the deck where a bucket of water was thrown over them. The decks were then thoroughly scrubbed and even in some cases dry-holystoned[11] as the surgeon-superintendents were concerned about the health of their charges. The bedding was rolled up and stowed away, and after breakfast, which was usually served at about 8 am, school assembled.

Many convicts who had not previously learnt to read or write did so on these voyages and those who could read were allowed to use the small libraries of religious and moral books. Those not attending classes picked oakum or sewed sacks on deck. Just before lunch the lemon or lime juice and sugar was passed round with the surgeon making sure that every man received some. Next the wine ration was given to each man and then followed lunch. School met again in the afternoon and after supper at about 4 pm exercise was taken. The prisoners were looped together in batches by chains, which ran through their leg-irons known as 'bazzels with chains'[12] and in this way they shuffled despondently around the deck. If the master and surgeon-superintendent were caring men they quite often struck the irons off during the voyage and allowed the prisoners the freedom to dance or play games during the exercise session.

The convicts had their hair cut every two weeks, were shaved twice a week and they were also expected to wash their own clothes. At sunset the men collected their bedding and were taken below where they were locked in for the night. In rough weather the convicts could be kept shut in for several days with the stench of humanity becoming more and more unpleasant. During the voyage of the *Edward* the surgeon noted in his journal that *'much rain fell and the weather was very unsettled'* so Richard Kear and his friends probably spent some of this time battened down in this floating hell.

By all accounts the convicts on board the *Edward* were a reasonably well behaved bunch, possibly due to the fact that the weather on their voyage did not allow them much freedom, but it was not always so. Many surgeon-superintendents were unable to keep their undisciplined charges in order and mutinies were quite common. *'We hear of an occasion upon which the convicts took possession of two of the ship's guns, and were proceeding to load them when the pieces were recaptured'*.[13] Many of the demoralised convicts became the most undisciplined and brutal prisoners and were eventually returned as an extra punishment to serve out their sentences on hulks in England.

The men from the Forest of Dean had never been on the ocean before and in between their bouts of seasickness they would have seen sights to amaze them. Porpoises tumbled through the towering Atlantic waves and tiny black and white storm petrels followed the wake of the ship to pick up any scraps of food thrown overboard. As the *Edward* drew nearer to her destination large patches of Gulf-weed often surrounded the ship and groups of 'Portuguese men-of-war' could be seen, *'beautiful little floating mollusks that cruise in these parts under their opaline sails of purple and rose-coloured membrane'*.[14]

On the 24th February 1853 the man at the masthead shouted the long awaited word 'Land'! and all the men craned forward for their first glimpse of Bermuda. They would have noticed first several low hummocks of land sharply defined against the sky. As he steered the ship towards the islands, the master of the *Edward*, John Adamson, would have taken particular note of reports warning against the sudden and violent storms which occur around Bermuda in the winter. *'Towards the end of the day, the entire horizon is obscured with heavy, black clouds; thunder and lightning are the advance warning of winds which follow later. When it begins to blow, it continually varies, with violent gusts at twenty or thirty minute intervals, during which are calms; the ocean becomes very rough and dangerous, especially for small vessels, because the direction of the waves is by no means regular'*.[15]

The *Edward* anchored at the north end of the island of Bermuda off Fort William to await the pilot ship, which was to guide them to their final destination. Most pilots were always on the lookout for approaching ships and immediately put to sea. Pilot boats were easily identifiable because of their peculiar construction, *'of a light draught of water forward, with a long heel or deep sternmost; rigged with one mast and bowsprit, carrying a triangular mainsail, a foresail, and jib, and occasionally, a gaff topsail and square-sail'*.[16] Government pilot boats had distinctive blue lines with white arrows on them. In 1830, pilots were paid at the rate of 3s. per day plus provisions and one dollar per foot for any government ship.

The weather was still unfavourable and it was not until the 26th of February that a small steamer came to tow the *Edward* along the coastline of Bermuda through the south channel. Bermuda is not one island but a long, curving archipelago of nearly 150 islands surrounded by treacherous reefs and so it was essential for men with local knowledge to steer a course avoiding these dangers.

In 1848 John Mitchel, an Irish political agitator, was imprisoned in the hulks of Bermuda before being banished to Van Diemens Land. In his journal he recorded his impressions of Bermuda as his ship was piloted through the same south channel during the month of June. *'Presently a boat came off: the boatmen were mulattoes, with palmetto hats; the pilot himself an utter negro. Soon we passed the dangerous entrance that lies between the easternmost island (crowned by a battery of Carthaginian cannon) and a great reef that bounds the archipelago on the north; and then we coasted along two of the largest islands for about ten miles, and had a clear view of the land, the houses and the people. Almost with glasses we might have inspected the domestic arrangements through their open doors.*

There is a thick population all along here: their houses are uniformly white, both walls and roof, but uncomfortable-looking for the want of chimneys; the cooking- house being usually a small detached building. The rocks, wherever laid bare (except those washed by the sea), are white or cream-coloured. The whole surface of the islands is made up of hundreds of low hillocks, many of them covered with a pitiful scraggy brush of cedars; and cedars are their only tree. The land not under wood is of a brownish green colour, and of a most naked and arid, hungry and thirsty visage. No wonder: for not one single stream, not one spring, rill, or well, gushes, trickles, or bubbles in all the three hundred isles, with their three thousand hills. The hills are too low, and the land too narrow, and all the rock is a porous calcareous concretion, which drinks up all the rain that falls on it, and would drink ten times as much, and be thirsty afterwards. Heavens! what a burned and blasted country. The people, it seems, have to be assiduous in catching the rain; cunning in spouts and tanks; and their stone is at any rate good for filtering water when they have it. I can see no cultivation of any sort, except some gardens; and there is very little of the land cultivated at all. On the whole, this place bears to my eyes an unkindly and foreign aspect; and as we coasted along here mile after mile, I saw nothing but the small hills and shrubby cedars, and parched soil'.

John Mitchel continued his description of Bermuda by reporting in his journal *'But, after all, these are fertile and fine islands'*. As he had earlier reported that there did not appear to be any cultivated land that he could see we can only presume that he was told, or had previously read, that parts of the island had an *'abundance of fruit, vegetables and fish'*. As his ship moved on down the coast and the scenery changed he finished by saying; *'I can see some cows, and plenty of goats, pigs, poultry. Verily, the land is a good land'*.

Although Richard Kear and the others were intrigued by what they saw it

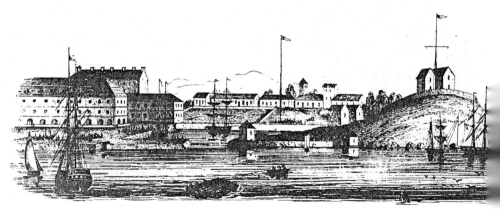

The Government Dockyard, Bermuda.

was another time when they must have felt a tinge of homesickness for the Forest of Dean with its canopy of trees and green glades. As the *Edward* moved slowly along the coast the convicts may have seen great shoals of brightly coloured fish darting amongst the reefs whilst overhead they may have caught sight of the strange bright yellow Kisskadee birds with their distinctive cry.

As the *Edward* rounded Spanish point the pilot boat had to negotiate some of the most treacherous waters surrounding the islands. '*Even with a fair wind to or from Ireland Island (on which the new dockyard is situated) ships are liable to strike upon the heads of rocks everywhere scattered about; this happened to a ship I was in, with a most expert pilot on board; the weather being cloudy, the rock spots did not show themselves sufficiently clear to be altogether avoided*'.[17] In 1864 nautical directions were published which describe this particular area. '*From Spanish Point to Ireland Island a ledge of rocks divides the Great Sound from Grassy Bay. There are two passages through this; one called the Stage Channel, near Sober Island, the North entrance; and one near Spanish Point; through these is the channel to Hamilton Harbour. There is also another line of reefs running between the North point of Somerset Island and the chain of islets South of Hamilton Harbour; this reef has also to be passed to enter the Great Sound South of which is Port Royal Bay, which has a depth across it for boats only…*'.[18]

At last the ship reached Grassy Bay in front of the government island where the dockyard was established. This island is at the extreme northwest of the whole group and is named Ireland Island. The convicts would have noticed the Commissioner's house first. A large square white building conspicuously set on a hill at the west end of the island. Below this a whole range of buildings crowned the hill in the middle of the island including the barracks for the soldiers and the government storehouses. The hill behind these buildings was cut into terraces mounted with cannon. This barrack hill connected with another hill on the extreme north of the island, which was occupied by other government buildings, all surrounded by powerful batteries. '*In the crescent formed by all*

these works, to the eastward, is the naval dockyard, with its stores, offices, and wet dock. Some of these are vast and sumptuous buildings'.[19]

The harbour itself was a very busy place during the mid-nineteenth century with ships moving in all directions making the scene a very lively one for the convicts who had just spent several weeks in the solitude of the ocean. The main dock was sheltered by a breakwater and inside this the convicts would have seen seven *'clumsy hulks, roofed over, and peopled by men in white linen blouses and straw hats, and on the back of every man's blouse, certain characters and figures, and the queen's broad arrow'.*[20] One of these hulks was to be home for Richard Kear for the next ten years.

On the 27th February 1853 just prior to disembarkation the surgeon William Rogers carried out the orders of the Acting Governor of Bermuda and made sure that the convicts *'were thoroughly washed with soap and hot water'*. He made an entry in his journal, which again shows that he was a man of some compassion. *'Sent 12 to hospital each that they required hospital treatment being as nearly all were complaining of debility. I deemed it advisable they should have a few days of quietitude before going on board the hulks'*. Apart from the convicts sent to hospital, William Rogers was able to conclude in his journal that 232 men had landed in good health.

1   PRO ADM 101/22/9 Surgeons journal of the *Edward*
2   *Ibid.*
3   *Ibid.*
4   National Maritime Museum, Manuscripts Section
5   'Hackmatack' from American Indian. The American larch or Tamarack (Larix Americana) found in the Northern swamps of the United States.
6   *The Convict Ships* - Bateson p. 91
7   *Ibid.* p. 65
8   *On the Winds and Navigation of the Bermudas* - Reid
9   PRO ADM 101/22/9 Surgeons journal of the *Edward*
10 *The Convict Ships* - Bateson pp. 66-67
11 *Ibid.* p. 80
12 *Ibid.* p. 74
13 *The English prison hulks* - Branch-Johnson
14 *Jail journal* - Mitchel
15 *Considérations Générales sur L'Océan Atlantique* - Kerhallet
16 *Directions for making the Bermudas 1803* - Downie,
17 *Description of the coasts of Bermuda* - Evans R.N.
18 *Description of the Bermudas or Somers Islands: with Nautical Directions* - Findlay FRGS.
19 *Jail journal* - Mitchel
20 *Ibid.* pp. 29-30

Chapter Eight

BERMUDA, A WORLD APART

Richard Kear and the other men from the Forest of Dean did not have time to ponder on the reason for their being sent to Bermuda, but if they had then they would have discovered that the British had colonised this group of islands back in the early seventeenth century.

The first known reference to the islands of Bermuda came not from an Englishman but a Spaniard named Juan Bermudez after whom the islands got their name. Juan Bermudez was a merchantman who, between 1495 and 1519 made several voyages across the Atlantic to the New World. Tradition has it that in 1503 as he headed a group of five ships home from America to Spain he sailed close to Bermuda and claimed it for the Spanish. The islands were first charted on the Peter Martyr map of 1511.[1] Bermudez had reported sightings of many reefs around the islands and this was confirmed by another Spaniard, Oviedo who tried to land there in 1515. Oviedo had the idea of leaving some hogs on Bermuda so that any shipwrecked men might have food, but the ship was unable to anchor owing to excessively strong winds. He did give one of the earliest descriptions of the land, saying that there was one large hill and he also noted that there were a great many birds. Oviedo was convinced that settlement on Bermuda would be very useful as a naval base in view of imminent attacks by the French, and in 1538 Captain Bartolomé Carreño was sent to report on the possibility of this. He discovered two deep-water harbours and plenty of palms, cedar trees and fish. He was troubled by the lack of fresh water and stated that survival would be difficult but not impossible. However, apart from short visits by groups of shipwrecked sailors forced to spend time there, Bermuda was not settled until much later.

By the middle of the sixteenth century Spanish ships were regularly using the route between the Gulf of Mexico and up through the Florida Strait to turn east past Bermuda. Although fleets were warned of the great dangers of the reefs, shipwrecks continued to occur and survivors wrote down many accounts of the islands. The French, too, used this shipping route and when one of their ships was wrecked on the treacherous reefs in 1556 a good account was given of how the crew survived. They caught turtles and birds to eat along with prickly pears and palm nuts and they used the native cedar wood to rebuild their ship.

The first Englishman to give an account of Bermuda was also in a shipwreck.

Henry May had been stranded in the Caribbean after the ship he was travelling on was wrecked. He managed to find passage on a French pirate ship returning home, and it was this ship which was wrecked on the North Rock of Bermuda. May described the cedar trees and plentiful fish of the islands and he spoke about wild hogs and the variety of birds. The hogs must have survived from some unknown shipwreck or perhaps Oviedo back in 1515 had managed to put a few animals ashore. Henry May did not think that the islands would be suitable for settlement, and this was re-iterated by Sir Walter Raleigh in 1596 when he described the Bermudas as '*a hellish sea for thunder, lightning and storms*'.[2] Another English sailor Samuel Champlain also seems to have passed Bermuda in extreme weather as he reported in about 1600, that the island '*is difficult to approach on account of the dangers that surround it. It almost always rains there, and thunder is so frequent, that it seems as if heaven and earth must come together. The sea is very tempestuous about the said island, and the waves as high as mountains*'.[3]

In 1603 five Spanish galleons disappeared in the Florida Strait but one was driven by bad weather on to a sandy beach of Bermuda, still today called Spanish Point. During the next twenty-two days whilst the crew endeavoured to repair and refloat the ship, the Captain, Diego Ramirez made a thorough exploration of the island. Ramirez produced the first manuscript map of the island and together with his pilot Hernando Muniz they noted descriptions of their surroundings. They spoke of the great number of cedar trees and palmettos and the lack of any fresh drinking water other than pools of rainwater. They relied for food on the herds of wild hogs, many varieties of fish and the nocturnal shearwaters (cahows) known as 'the devils of Bermuda' from their cries. Ramirez was able to report that there were two good harbours, one at the Great Sound where his ship had come aground and a second at St. Georges. On returning to Spain, Ramirez's report was handed over to the Spanish government to look at the possibility for the colonisation of Bermuda, but Philip III was disinterested and before he could think more about it events occurred which were to change the course of history.

An English fleet of nine ships, under the command of Admiral Sir George Somers, set sail for Jamestown, Virginia on the 2nd June 1609 with food for the starving colony. As the fleet reached the islands of Bermuda they were struck by a hurricane and the admiral's ship the *Sea Venture* was thrown onto the rocks and wrecked. Somers guided the battered ship to her final resting-place on a coral reef off St. Georges harbour. Among the survivors who finally reached land were the new governor of Virginia, Sir Thomas Gates, and the captain of the *Sea Venture*, Christopher Newport. For the next ten months the shipwrecked crew busied themselves building two small ships in which to continue their journey to Virginia. The two ships, to be called *Deliverance* and *Patience* were constructed from the native cedar wood and equipment salvaged from the *Sea Venture*. Sir George Somers became the hero of the men; keeping spirits high and proving that survival was possible on Bermuda.

The Virginia Company said in a report prepared in 1610 that Somers and the crew had lived well on *'the berries of* Cedar, *the* Palmeto *tree, the prickle pear, sufficient fish, plenties of Tortoises, and divers kinds, which sufficed to sustaine nature'.*[4] Somers sailed a small boat right round the islands and made quite a detailed map and he instigated tests on the fertility of the ground to see if it would be possible to grow crops. When the time came to continue the voyage a few members of the crew were left behind on Bermuda to tend to the herds of wild pigs roaming the islands, and after a few months in Virginia Sir George Somers returned to Bermuda for some fresh supplies of pork for the colony. There he died and the islands were for many years after called the Somers Isles.

A brief statement on the episode in Bermuda, probably by Sir Thomas Gates, was also included in the 1610 report of the Virginia Company. It said of Bermuda *'These Islands of the Bermudos, have ever been accounted as an inchanted pile of rocks, and a desert inhabitation for Divils, but all the Fairies of the rocks were but flockes of birdes, and all the Divils that haunted the woods, were but herds of swine'.*[5]

The stories about the ill-fated shipwreck spread throughout England and it certainly caught the imagination of one William Shakespeare who based his last play *The Tempest* on the reported events. Survivors of the shipwreck spoke of *'a great wealth of pearls at that island'* and together with the news from Sir George Somers that survival would be possible on Bermuda, the Virginia Company held a meeting to discuss the future of the islands. *'The state and hope of the Bermoodes was there fully dyscust And Concluded to send a Collony thither, the place so opulent, fertile and pleasant that all men were willing to go there'.*[6]

For some considerable time it had been the desire of England to have its own source of tropical fruits, which were only available from Spain, France and the other Atlantic Islands. Virginia had proved unsuccessful in growing these fruits and now with the prospect of a colony which might produce such products, the Virginia Company was awarded a land grant by King James the first and they set about the colonisation of Bermuda. On the 11th July 1612 the *Plough* arrived at St. Georges harbour with some fifty to sixty men, women and children. Settlement by the English had begun.

For the first few years conditions were hard as the local resources soon ran out and information that the Spanish wanted Bermuda for themselves worried the first governor Richard More. In 1612 two Spanish ships made a reconnaissance of the islands and More was forced to scare them away with one of the two guns he had salvaged from the wreck of the *Sea Venture*. Despite the hardship more settlers arrived from England and two successive governors, Daniel Tucker and Nathaniel Butler, built eight forts as protection. In 1614 the Virginia Company sold its rights to the islands to the newly formed Bermuda Company for £2,000, and in 1616 the islands were surveyed and divided into

The Bermuda Islands taken from the
Bermuda Weekly Dispatch, 1870

25 acre plots to be known as parishes. Each investor in the Bermuda Company had a parish named after him and was allowed 50 acres. The expected export of exotic fruits never materialised, instead it was tobacco and sugar cane which proved the saviour of the settlers. In 1616 slaves were brought from the West Indies, to dive for pearls and to harvest the crops.

During the rest of the seventeenth century the colonists expanded their exports by going into the whaling business to provide oil, which was well paid for in England. They also discovered that the Turks Islands some thousand miles to the south of Bermuda were so hot and dry that they proved ideal for the production of salt from the sea. This salt was traded in American ports for much needed food and the trading continued until the Turks Islands were taken over by the Bahamas in 1799.

In 1684 another era ended when the Bermuda Company, after a five-year battle, finally lost its independent charter and became a British colony. The first governor appointed by the Crown was Sir Robert Robinson and he settled in St. Georges, then the capital of Bermuda. Henry Curson in 1699 produced a compendium in which he gave descriptions of all the dominions, plantations and territories belonging to England. In his description of Bermuda he states that *'the Air is almost constantly Clear, (Except when it Thunders and Lightens) is extream Temperate and Healthful, few dying of any Disease but Age; so that many remove from England hither only to enjoy a long healthful Life, and after having continued there, are fearful of Removing out of so pure an Air'.* To further encourage potential settlers he continued *'the very Spiders here are not Venemous, but of divers curious Colours, and make their Web so strong, that oftentimes small Birds are entangled and caught therein. Their Cedar Trees are different from all others, and the Wood very sweet'.*[7] Certainly by the time Curson wrote this description there were well over 3000 English settlers in Bermuda.

A Bermudian boat.

Bermuda's staunch royalists had to face the most difficult test of their loyalties in 1775 when the American Continental Congress announced a trade embargo against all colonies retaining an attachment to the Crown. King George the third forbade Bermuda to trade with Washington's rebels causing despair for the inhabitants of Bermuda who relied heavily on their close personal ties with Virginia and other American colonies for food. Bermuda negotiated to provide salt to the Americans in exchange for the lifting of the embargo but the rebellious colonies stated that they would only lift the sanctions in return for gunpowder. Unknown to the Governor George Bruere, a group of Bermudans broke into the magazine at St. Georges and stole the island's whole supply of gunpowder, which they delivered to the Americans. George Washington at once lifted the embargo and thanked the people of Bermuda for their assistance. Fortunately Bermuda had a chance to win back some glory for the Crown when later in the war her privateers captured dozens of American ships.

After the United States of America gained independence in 1783, Great Britain lost all its naval bases in the American colonies. Britain began to discuss Bermuda's potential as a defence asset and Captain Thomas Hurd, a hydrographer, was sent out to chart the waters round the islands. His very detailed survey in 1791 showed possible anchorages which would be deep enough for the Royal Navy. Two particularly large sites were situated off the north side of St. Georges Island and at Grassy Bay, part of the Great Sound, to the west of Bermuda near a rocky headland known as Ireland Island. Rear Admiral Sir George Murray, a man of great vision, saw at once the potential of a naval depot at St. Georges and a fortified dockyard at Ireland Island and in 1795 he applied for approval to purchase several tracts of land and small islands for the Crown. Sadly before his plans could be implemented he died on return to England in 1798.

Renewed fighting between Great Britain and France meant that British ships had to be protected in the western Atlantic and it was decided to use Bermuda as a base for the Royal Navy. The anchorage at St. Georges became home for the British fleet and many small Bermuda cedar vessels were built there, especially during the Napoleonic wars. Bermuda shipping excelled all others for speed and after the Battle of Trafalgar a Bermuda sloop was chosen as the fastest way to get the news of the victory back to England. With the threat from Napoleon still hanging over England, it became even more important to establish a permanent naval base in Bermuda and in 1808 Sir George Murray's original proposals were resurrected and a new survey undertaken, this time by Admiral Sir John Borlase Warren. It was decided that the harbour at St. Georges would not remain suitable for the larger vessels now required and for security the Great Sound offered the best possibilities.

Ireland Island was purchased in June 1809 for the sum of £4,800 for the establishment of the Royal Naval Dockyard. Captain Carr, who in 1893 kept a book of naval history, wrote about the name Ireland Island, pointing out that a Mr. Ireland, an influential inhabitant of the Sandys parish in 1623, had undoubtedly given his name to this island at the extreme northwest of Bermuda.

At the same time as Warren bought Ireland Island he also bought several smaller islands in the Great Sound making sure that the valuable cedar trees on each of them remained. The trees were bought separately by the Admiralty and proved extremely useful in the building of the new dockyard. Before the purchase of this new site for the naval dockyard the island was a jungle of cedar and sage, over-run by wild pigs. A small community lived in wooden houses thatched with palmetto and only made contact with the rest of Bermuda when they rowed their boats across the Great Sound to the main island. Faced with the challenge of creating a naval base from this rocky outcrop Warren set about erecting buildings wherever he could fit them in. Much of the soft local stone was unsuitable for building work and many of the early constructions were built of wood. The Royal Engineers were responsible for the initial building work and a small guard unit of an officer and 20 marines was formed to protect the stores. Warren housed these men in an old ship, known as a hulk, which had been used for stores at St. Georges. Funds from the British government poured into Bermuda for the building work and before long the Great Storehouse together with accommodation for the officers and workers had been erected.

The new dockyard had scarcely begun to take shape when in 1812 war broke out between England and America. During the earlier American War of Independence Bermudans had been divided in their loyalties but this time they firmly supported England. The Royal Navy used St. Georges harbour for their fleet, and Bermuda privateers were responsible for the capture of 300 vessels. The war ended in 1815 with neither side claiming victory but it had shown the advantage of Bermuda's strategic position. Work began again in earnest to fortify the islands and continue work on the Imperial Dockyard. In the same year that the war ended members of the Colonial Parliament met in the small town hall in the new town of Hamilton and decided that with the shift of activity to the western side of Bermuda it would be sensible to move the capital. The St. Georgians were not at all pleased by this decision but from 1815 Hamilton became the new capital of Bermuda.

The Royal Engineers continued to supervise the building work at the dockyard using local labour and any slaves that were available. The first stone building was the guardhouse erected in about 1812 of soft Bermuda stone, and this was followed by storehouses and other residences built of the same stone. Gradually between 1820-1850s all these buildings were pulled down and rebuilt using the hard limestone blasted from a quarry on Ireland Island. Captain Thomas Cunningham of the Royal Engineers was asked to provide a scheme to *'secure the permanent military possession of the Bermuda Islands'*[8] and he first proposed that a large ditch be cut across Ireland Island to guard against any land attack. He also proposed a martello tower and a three-gun tower to the east of the island. By the time he left Bermuda in 1816 only the ditch had been started and the whole building work was falling way behind schedule.

It was still thought very important to press ahead with the construction of the dockyard and during the next two years the hurried early building was replaced by a more methodical approach, backed up by ample funding by the Crown and a new detachment of Royal Engineers sent out to augment the local labour. Rennie's estimate drawn up in 1818 which included a victualling yard, a dry dock and a breakwater, added up to a staggering £648,548.[9] It was to be 1870 before a floating dry dock was towed out from England but work was put in hand to provide residences, wharves and the harbour.

Captain John Lewis had been appointed as the first resident commissioner and in 1822, to add to the already heavy workload, plans were drawn up for a house for him. The true cost of the building of this house never seems to have been established but expenditure on the dockyard between 1822 and 1830 shows the commissioner's house costing £37,805.[10] The house was certainly one of the most lavish to have been built in a dockyard, and its site on high ground at the north end of Ireland Island commanded magnificent views. Designed by Holl, the two-storey house was built of local stone with wide roofed verandas on three sides. To supplement the local building materials, the roof members and veranda supports, which were made of cast iron, were all prefabricated in England and together with some of the architectural stonework were shipped out to Bermuda at vast expense.

It was necessary to clear several sites before buildings could be erected in the dockyard area and although gunpowder helped to blast away the rock the lack of local labour made progress painfully slow. Late in 1823, Robert Peel sent word from the Home Office in England that prisoners would be sent out to Bermuda to help with the building work. Transportation overseas or hard labour on defence work and harbour construction within the United Kingdom had traditionally dealt with overcrowding in English prisons and Bermuda was considered very suitable for combining both these forms of punishment.

Royal Naval Dockyard, Bermuda, with the clocktowers and in the distance the imposing bulk of the commissioner's house. 1997.   Averil Kear

Anthony Trollope visited Bermuda in 1858 and thought; '*at such a place works may be done by convict labour which could not be done otherwise*'. He felt that the hard work they would be expected to carry out should be a punishment '*sharp, hard to bear, heavy to body and mind, disagreeable in all ways so that the world at large may know and see, and clearly acknowledge, – even the uneducated world, – that honesty* is *the best policy*'.[11] Although he was sure that the idea of sending rogues and ruffians and the worst type of criminals to Bermuda was a good one as it got rid of them from the shores of England, he was not at all sure that up to 1858 the results had been entirely successful.

It was not the first time that convicts had been transported to Bermuda, as in 1799 the hulk *Somerset* had arrived in St. Georges and moored in what is still called Convict Bay. This batch of prisoners was used for local building work although this was not then connected with the navy. In 1823, just after Peel's report, 20 officers of the Royal Marines and 393 enlisted soldiers were sent out to Bermuda to prepare the convict establishment. In February 1824, *H.M.S. Antelope* sailed in to Grassy Bay bringing the first 300 convicts to work on the dockyard. These first convicts were put to work immediately and with nothing more than a pick and shovel they began to build yards, accommodation blocks, shore defences and batteries, which would eventually result in one of the most highly fortified of all overseas naval stations.

With a new influx of convicts in 1824 work began in earnest on the building of the keep and casemate barracks.[12] The prisoners were housed in two aged men-of-war ships brought out to Bermuda and converted into floating prisons, the *Dromedary* which was used until at least 1848 and the *Coromandel* which had for many years sailed with convicts to Australia. The Great Wharf and the walls of the north yard began to take shape and the breakwater was growing at the rate of thirteen feet per month. Convicts who were sent out to Bermuda were not all hardened criminals; many were skilled men such as architects and engineers who because of petty fraud or theft had been sentenced to six years in the hulks. Their skills were put to good use and in return many of them were given reduced sentences and returned to England.

Transport ships brought still more convicts to Bermuda together with Royal Navy hulks to be used as store ships. The *Tenedos* was used as a prison ship until 1848 when she was turned into the hospital hulk. The Commissioner's house was finished and work was pressing ahead on the northeast end of the yard. Then in 1836 a devastating hurricane hit Bermuda and the new breakwater was severely damaged in three places. Many boats were sunk in the storm and the ongoing construction of the dockyard was delayed considerably as the workers had to concentrate all their efforts on repair work. It was estimated that the cost of the damage amounted to £30,000 and between 1837 and 1848 hardly any new construction work was carried out on the dockyard.

The Earl of Dundonald arrived in Bermuda in 1848 to take over as Commander in Chief and sent a report back to the Admiralty complaining that

Royal Naval Dockyard, Bermuda. A view towards the Casemates Prison. 1997.   Averil Kear

The clocktowers, Royal Naval Dockyard, Bermuda. 1997.   Averil Kear

The dockyard gates. 1997.   Averil Kear

The Watergate. 1997.   Averil Kear

'there was nothing in the Yard to defend – the space enclosed by ramparts is an entire void, except the half finished Victualling Store, and two small wooden buildings to be pulled down. The space is incapable of holding the Dockyard and Victualling Yard. There is not a Shed in which the Sails of the Flag Ship can be fitted, not even space for setting up a Spunyarn reel out of the rays of the Sun. Water cannot be got for the Ships; the glacis should be plastered and tanks built'.[13]
Dundonald commented on the sheer extravagance of the commissioner's house and pointed out that if naval men had been involved with the original planning of the dockyard, then many thousands of pounds would have been saved. Under his energetic command work on the dockyard resumed and more convicts were sent out from England to join the other prisoners on the vastly overcrowded hulks in Grassy Bay.

The Royal Navy sent the *Medway* out to Bermuda in 1848 to act as yet another storeship but the need for accommodation for the convicts soon changed her use. Richard Kear and the others were to get to know the *Medway* very well over the next ten years.

[1] *Bermuda in the age of exploration and early settlement* - Quinn - p.41
[2] *Ibid.* p. 11
[3] *Ibid.* p. 11
[4] *Ibid.* p. 16
[5] *Ibid.* p. 16
[6] *Ibid.* p. 17
[7] *A compendium of the laws and government of England, Scotland and Ireland* - Curson
[8] *Bermuda Forts* - Harris p. 183
[9] *The Royal Dockyards* - Coad p. 367
[10] *Ibid.* p. 369
[11] *The West Indies and the Spanish Main* - Trollope p. 290
[12] The word 'casemate' for long used in Bermuda when referring to the barracks built at the southern end of the dockyard, in fact refers to chambers housing guns built into the rampart walls.
[13] *The Andrew and the Onions* - Stranack p. 14

Chapter Nine

HULKS and HARD LABOUR

Richard Kear and George Charles had been very seasick during the last part of the voyage of the *Edward* and were put aboard the hospital ship *Tenedos* to recover before being set to work in the dockyard. The other men, Thomas James, James James, Hiram Archer and Henry Shapcott were immediately sent to a prison ship, the old *Medway* hulk, to join the other 560 or so prisoners.

Pitcher, a small shipbuilder at Northfleet in Kent, had built the *Medway* during the Napoleonic wars. She was made of good English oak and originally carried 74 guns.[1] Her overall measurement was 176ft. x 49ft., the former being that of the gun-deck, and her tonnage was given as 1,768bm (builder's measurement) which in 1812 was a capacity arrived at by calculating the number of casks (tuns) of wine that the ship could carry. The *Medway* served nobly until by 1847, stripped of all her guns and looking decidedly battered, she was pensioned off and sent to Bermuda as a store ship. By 1848 she was refitted to accommodate the ever-increasing number of convicts being sent out from Great Britain and Ireland. At the time the Forest of Dean men arrived the crew of the *Medway* consisted of the overseer John Kirkham, together with four mates, seventeen

Convict Hulk Medway *at the 'Short Arm', Ireland Island c. 1855.*   courtesy Chris Addams

Convict Hulk Dromedary.   courtesy Chris Addams

guards, five quartermasters and a boy of fifteen years old who was the clerk, his name was William Kirkham, the son of the overseer.

There were three other hulks housing prisoners in 1853, the *Dromedary*, which was eventually sold to a Mr. Murphy in Bermuda in 1866, the *Coromandel*, which having been brought to Bermuda in 1827 was finally broken up at the end of 1853, and the *Thames*. The *Thames* had originally been moored at St. Georges where there was an outbreak of Yellow Fever on board at the beginning of

Comptroller and Convicts, Bermuda, 1860.
Mitchell Library, Share Library and New South Wales PXA 280. f.3

Tenedos, *Convict Hospital Ship*   courtesy Chris Addams

1853, and even when she was eventually moved to Grassy Bay convicts swore that they could still smell the fever on board her. She finally sank at her moorings in 1863.

The *Tenedos* arrived in Bermuda in 1843 and was used as the hospital ship from 1848. She was anchored near Boaz Island taking patients who had originally been housed at the Royal Naval hospital. She was broken up in 1863 when the last convicts were sent home. Two hulks used as storeships, the *Weymouth* and the *Royal Oak* were also moored in Grassy Bay, but after the victualling yard was completed at the dockyard in 1853, the *Royal Oak* was taken to pieces and the *Weymouth* was sent to St. Georges for dredging work.

Drawing of a scene by the convict hulk, Coromandel.   courtesy Chris Addams

The convict hulk Weymouth.   courtesy Chris Addams

Severe overcrowding of these aged prison hulks forced the Crown to purchase Boaz and Watford Islands from the Royal Navy in 1848. Convicts were set to work to build barracks on these islands linked to Ireland Island, and in 1851, 600 prisoners were transferred there but the majority of the unfortunate men were left to the squalid conditions of the hulks. *'Between 1823 and 1861, 9,094 convicts served in Bermuda, 2,041 of whom died from ailments contracted as a direct result of their conditions of service'.*[2]

As soon as Richard Kear and George Charles had recovered from their seasickness, they were sent to join the other men on board the *Medway* hulk. Kear was given the prison number 2046, George Charles number 2048, James James number 2047, Thomas James, number 2045, Henry Shapcott number 2055 and Hiram Archer, number 2056. All the men were issued with the regulation clothing of three brown holland smock frocks, three pairs of coarse canvas trousers, two cotton shirts, two flannel shirts, three pairs of shoes, two handkerchiefs and one straw hat.

On the 15th November 1847 the officers on board the hulks were especially asked to note *'Prisoners in the probationary period will have a mark (arrow) conspicuously placed on their frocks both before and behind'.*[3] *The Illustrated London News* commented on the clothes worn by the convicts in an article written on the 17th June 1848, making special note of the issue of flannel shirts and drawers saying that they were *'necessary to absorb the excessive perspiration engendered by exposure to the rays of a tropical sun'.* Another ruling issued by Charles Elliot, the Governor of the convict establishment, again referred to the two flannel shirts issued to each convict. Overseers of the hulks were directed to keep one shirt in store to prevent *'sale and traffic of clothing by Prisoners amongst themselves and other persons'.* In order to obtain a fresh shirt the convicts had to return one to the store *'scrubbed and dry',*[4] thus ensuring even wear of both. Listings of clothing and personal supplies for the entire convict establishment for the year April 1853-1854 give interesting details, which include:–

3,500 duck frocks	1,800 duck trousers	1,800 handkerchiefs
1,800 cotton shirts	8,000 flannel shirts	1,000 lbs. shoe leather
150 lbs. of shoe hemp	100 lbs. of thread	1 gross combs
1 gross scissors	2,000 yards of dowlas	2,000 iron spoons[5]

Convicts transported to Bermuda came from all walks of life and some were allowed to wear their own clothes, which were packed away on arrival when they were issued with prison clothing. The clothes were returned on release unless the convict died, in which case the clothes were auctioned. One such auction took place on the 6th June 1854 and raised about £10. The clothes belonged to a deceased convict from the *Medway* hulk, who may well have been known to Richard Kear and the others. The following list of the deceased man's clothing shows a life-style in sharp contrast to his final days at the Bermuda Dockyard:–

black cloth overcoat	blue frock coat	shepherd plaid frock coat
blue cloth trousers	plaid trousers	blue cloth vest
2 black flowered vests	flowered satin vest	plaid vest
striped vest	4 white shirts	2 check shirts
2 silk handkerchiefs	2 black satin ties	1 cap
wellington boots	7 pairs of cotton socks	silver watch guard
tooth brush	shaving brush	6 hand towels[6]

Convict dress on Bermuda.
Illustrated London News 17th June 1848

Varying accounts of the accommodation provided for the convicts depended on who was reporting the conditions. John Mitchel who was held prisoner between 1848 and 1849 on the *Dromedary* hulk described his quarters as *'a sort of cavern, just a little higher and a little wider than a dog-house … quite dark but for two very small and dim bulls'-eyes that are set into the deck above'*. Mitchel was unable to stand upright and the only furniture was one wooden stool. There was a hammock to sleep on which had to be slung diagonally to fit the area, which was about six-foot square. William Sydes, a convict on board the *Coromandel* between 1838 and 1845 said, *'there was not*

Public Records Office HO 8/118

Medway Hulk prison register, 31st December 1853.

room for one half of the ships company to hang their hammocks up in decent manner, one half of them lay three deep and naked'. At night after the doors were locked the only light was by a piece of candle left on a ledge, and again Mitchel's description brings a shudder. *'The light of the candle showed me a great many big brown cockroaches, nearly two inches long, running with incredible speed over the walls and floor'*. Apart from candles, which were issued at the rate of one ton for every hundred men on board per month, the *Medway* was allowed six lamps in total to burn between decks at night using two gills of whale oil for each lamp per week.[7]

The weather in Bermuda played a large part in determining the living conditions of the men. In the winter months the temperature was between 55°F – 70°F but high, blustery winds made it feel much cooler and in the summer it was not uncommon for the temperature to reach 90°F and hurricanes sometimes occurred. A report by the Rev. J. M. Guilding, chaplain on one of the hulks in 1859, stated; *'the heat between the decks is so oppressive as to make the stench intolerable, and to cause the miserable inmates frequently to strip off every vestige of clothing and gasp at the portholes for a breath of air'*. The humidity, combined with this extreme heat, was responsible for many illnesses and tempers of both convicts and guards flared often.

In contrast to the awful conditions portrayed by the convicts John Mitchel and William Sydes, three surprise visits to the hulks in 1860 by Governor Freeman Murray told a different story. On very hot nights during June and July he noted *'I made a thorough examination and saw every convict, whether in his hammock, in separate confinement, or in hospital. I was surprised at the perfect order and regularity exhibited, after the picture drawn by Chaplain Guilding of the supposed condition of the hulks at night. The ventilation was good, the different decks free from close or impure smells, and so little oppressive was the heat,* (on the lowest deck of the *Medway* the temperature was 84 degrees on the hottest of the three nights) *that it would hardly be possible to find any establishment of the sort in better order'*.[8] Governor Murray commented further on the account of conditions given by the chaplain saying *'I can only hope that he has been enormously imposed upon by the accounts of some of the prisoners'*. He went on to say that *'the conditions of the inmates is vastly superior to that of the crews of any of Her Majesty's ships'* and that *'the convicts are remarkably healthy, and the hulks kept in a most remarkable state of cleanliness, which is sufficient proof that the Chaplain's estimate of the suffering's of those unfortunate men is founded on erroneous information'*.[9]

So much information had to be passed to London over the forty years that the Convict Establishment was in existence that it would have been very difficult for successive governors to send false reports. Although it cannot be said that conditions were ideal for Richard Kear and the others, at least they were housed, fed, clothed, and medically and spiritually cared for. One convict, John Morgan who was returned to England in 1847 after serving his sentence, reported that he was better off in Bermuda and if he found himself on hard times again then he would again steal in order to be transported.[10]

The convicts' day started early at 5 am. Firstly, under strict supervision they washed themselves and cleaned their cells and then breakfasted between 6.30 – 7.10 am. On that first morning Richard Kear would have found time to study his fellow prisoners on board the *Medway*. The men he was to spend the next ten years with were a mixed bunch. They were all clean-shaven with close-cropped hair and *'at first glance they look like the untransported population at home; but closer examination makes you aware that many of them have evil countenances and amorphous skulls'*.[11] Some of the prisoners, especially the young men, were given women's names, *'whether from their effeminate appearance or not, I will not pretend to say, but there are horrible things said of them'*[12] and their company was sought at night by many of the convicts. These same young men who had been forced into a life of crime back home, were sent to Bermuda in the vain hope that they would be reformed. They soon became *'initiated into mysteries and profound depths of corruption that their mother tongue has no name for'* and became as depraved as the rest of the men. Some of the men read profane books at the mess table and all of them seemed *'to cram as much brutal obscenity and stupid blasphemy into their common speech as it will hold'*.[13]

Charles Elliot, the governor in 1849, had issued a general instruction to the whole convict establishment about cursing and swearing in which he said *'I admonish the prisoners to consider that wicked and shameful speech is a vice rather of depraved habits than deliberate forethought but the indulgence in it sustains a degraded tone of feeling and a hardened conscience which it is their highest duty and interest to correct'*. He ordered that his message should be read out at divine service on the next Sunday in the misguided hope that the men would reform their evil ways of speaking. As expected, the order had no effect and the men from the Forest of Dean who would have been well used to rough speech would have joined in with the other inmates.

One of the worst criminals to be held in the convict establishment during the time the Forest of Dean men were there was an Irishman named Kirwan. Stories were told that human bones had been found when his garden in Ireland was dug up and, even worse, that he had dissected and made anatomical drawings of parts of the body of his own mother. The judge would not believe that anyone could do such a thing to his own mother but there was enough evidence to show that he had murdered his wife together with the wife of a Mr. Bowyer. He was first sent to Spike Island, the notorious Irish prison and then on to Bermuda. A lady who knew him well described him as; *'A man about middle height, strong and coarse, with a bad and determined expression of face and a soft oily voice'*. On his arrival in Bermuda, a long-term housebreaker was forced to relinquish his renowned first place in the criminal pack saying; *'I concede that honour to Mr. William Burke Kirwan'*. Surprisingly, Kirwan was put to work in the doctor's shop helping to make up the medicine. A prisoner who had returned to Ireland was asked what Kirwan was doing now and the reply came back that he had been put out of the doctor's shop, because *'He gave a prisoner, that he didn't like, some pills that didn't agree with him'*.[14]

After breakfast, the convicts spent about half an hour in chapel, listening to small bits read from the prayer book by the chaplain, before being taken by ferry from the hulk to their various workstations. Many of the convicts had to work shackled by ball and chain and those prisoners housed in the new shore prison on Boaz Island had to walk about two miles to the dockyard before beginning their day's work. John Mitchel was able to see the whole dockyard complex from the window of his cell and wrote in his journal *'upon the breakwater, which is also in part visible from my window, is another muster, sad to see: many hundreds of poor convicts marched in gangs, some of them in chains, to their work, in the quarries, or the new government buildings. They walk, as I fancy, with a drooping gait and carriage. Their eyes, it is said, are greatly injured by the glare of the white rocks, and many grow "moon- blind" as they call it, so that they stumble over stones as they walk'.*

The convicts were employed on various works, such as blasting, hewing and sawing stone from the quarries and other general building work. Other men were needed as carpenters and smiths and still more worked on the maintenance and repair of the hulks and other ships. The miners from the Forest of Dean were no strangers to work in quarries and would probably have been chosen for this work because of their experience. Most of the work handed out was heavy and hard but even infirm prisoners were given light work to do which was still of use to the establishment; this included mat work, rope work, brush and basketwork. In June 1860, a report shows the Royal Engineers supervising 2,445 convicts who were constructing a drawbridge leading to the *Medway* hulk, building a storehouse, limewashing the commissioner's house, and repairing roads. Another 500 convicts were working as carpenters in the mast and timber stores, building and repairing the naval storehouses, workmen's cottages and factory buildings and cutting rock in the quarries.[15] Richard Kear may well have been taken off work in the quarry for a while at the end of 1853, to help cut and stack the wood resulting from the breaking up of the *Coromandel* hulk.

On board a hulk.

101

Cutting stone.

Under the watchful eye of a convict officer the men worked until 12 noon when they stopped for lunch. In order to gain the maximum amount of effort from the convicts the British and Bermudan authorities made sure that the diet was satisfactory. All the provisions were sent from England with the exception of the soft bread, fresh beef and vegetables that were imported from the United States. Initially everything was stored in the two store ships, which meant that food deteriorated quickly in the damp humid conditions, but in 1853 the new victualling store was finished giving dry secure storage for supplies. During an average week in 1860 rations for each convict consisted of:

10 lb. of soft bread	$1^1/2$ lb. biscuit
4 lb. fresh beef	$1^1/2$ lb. salt pork
7 lb. vegetables	4 oz. oatmeal or barley
$1^1/2$ oz. tea	$5^1/2$ oz. chocolate
$10^1/2$ oz. sugar	$3^1/2$ gills of rum[16]

In 1859 when Anthony Trollope visited Bermuda's convict establishment he commented that the convict was very well provided for with good meat to eat whilst the native Bermudans had to chew on 'tough carcasses'. He was sure that the convicts had more than enough to eat particularly mentioning the bread ration saying, '*the amount may be of questionable advantage, as he cannot eat it all; but he probably sells it for drink*'. To try and save some money during 1852 the diet was varied to include salt cod on a Friday instead of the beef. It was suggested that the proportion of Irish convicts who were mostly Roman Catholic would especially welcome this. The officers and guards would have eaten a more substantial diet than the convicts, often being served with fish from around the islands. John Mitchel spoke of an '*abundance of good fish here, mullet, bonetto, a thick sort of flat-fish, and a red-fleshed fish not very much worse than salmon*'.

The major concern on Bermuda had always been the lack of fresh water for drinking, as there were no natural sources at all. Convicts and inhabitants alike had to depend on rainwater collected in giant tanks. The unusual terraced rooftops of the houses in Bermuda were constructed of cream-coloured blocks of coral-limestone cut into thin slabs which were then whitewashed on completion. The terraces channelled the rainwater into drainpipes connected to rounded or rectangular water tanks, which during the 19th century were situated above ground.

Around 1.30 pm the convicts returned to work. Some continued with the heavy work in the quarries but a report of progress of convict works at the dockyard for the month of May 1854 shows how diverse their work could be. Many fine schooners were built at Bermuda and still more ships passed by the Grassy Bay anchorage on their way to the United States of America or the West Indies. All these ships needed repairs and the ready-made convict workforce was made available.

I. Under Boatswain of the Yard:

H.M. Schooner *Bermuda*, heaving down to copper bottom	15 men
H.M. Steam Vessel *Kite*, disconnecting and taking out machinery	7 men
Victualling Establishment, cleaning cooperage	3 men
Receiving naval stores from Amazon store ship, and coals from *Polka, Charlotte, Ellen Sophia*, coal ships	292 men
Buoys and Beacons, in anchor hoy, shifting channel buoys	31 men
Store, making and repairing colours, cleaning and painting chains and blocks	45 men
Incidentals: attending in sheds, removing coals and cleaning coal sheds, yard, temporary chapel, and slip etc.	65 men

II. Under Shipwright's Dept:

H.M. Schooner *Bermuda*, caulking, coppering, making and fitting bitts, iron work, awning stanchions, and fire hearth	59 men
H.M. Steam Vessel *Kite*, disconnecting and taking out machinery	68 men
Commissariat Dept; coppering bottom, fitting and repairing *Wellington*, sailing boat	8 men
H.M. Receiving Ship *Weymouth*, cleaning and whitewashing slip	34 men

Convict Dept:

Medway hulk, caulking	17 men
Cleaning fire engines, diving apparatus, and repairing harnesses for yard horses	29 men
Buoys and Beacons, employed in shifting channel buoys	6 men
Fitting and painting of 12-foot dinghy, and making rowing crutches for Bermuda schooner, issuing and restowing wood materials	46 men
Sent to yard, as carters on new works	32 men
Removing stores from shipwright's shed to cooperage	13 men
Curlew, mail steam packet, making good defects of steam pipe	3 men

Receiving coal from coal barques, *Charlotte* and *Ellen Sophia,* and from brig *Polka*	406 men
Cleaning yard, workshops, sheds, square, and attending burial ground	56 men
Incidentals, heating steam and pitchboilers, and attending on yard horses as drivers	96 men[17]

The convicts were paid for the work they carried out at the rate of threepence per day. One penny was taken out for food and another for clothing. The commissariat held the third penny until the prisoner was released when the accumulated sum was handed over to him. As the list above shows, many of the convicts received very good training for all sorts of occupations and a great number of them used their new skills to find work when returning home after the end of their sentence.

Apart from two religious services on a Sunday, the prisoners spent half a day each week in school. Under the supervision of the chaplain most of the illiterate men learnt to read and write and the others extended their knowledge with lessons in geography, arithmetic, grammar, dictation and reading. In 1859 the daily average attending school on the *Medway* hulk was 58 and in December of that year a schoolmaster's report for the same hulk showed that only fifteen prisoners could neither read nor write, 89 could read only, 191 could read and write only imperfectly, 113 could read and write well, and 95 were well instructed.[18] Those who could read had access to the library containing some 1,500 books and those who could write were allowed to send letters home every three or four months when the mail steamer came through.

Richard Kear wrote home to his parents in their cottage at Oldcroft in the Forest of Dean but it would have taken a considerable time for his letters to reach them. He may not have received many letters back from them, as they had never had the opportunity to learn how to write. However, one letter, which someone must have written for Richard's mother Mary, was to let her son know that his father had died. Richard Kear senior died on the 16th December 1858 and in his will, which he wrote just two days before he died, he left everything to his wife stating that after her decease all his property should go to '*my son Richard Kear now residing at Bermuda West India*'. His will continued with legacies to his three daughters, Jane, Eliza and Harriet and finished by making provision for his property '*in case my said son Richard Kear do not return to England*'. This provision stated that after the death of his wife, his granddaughter Phoebe Ann Kear should receive the rent from his property until she reached twenty-one, at which point, if Richard had still not returned from Bermuda, the property was to be sold and the proceeds divided between his other children. In the glaring sun on board the *Medway*, Richard Kear must have been saddened by the knowledge that he would now never see his father again but pleased to know that his young daughter Phoebe was so well thought of by his parents.

The following year Richard again received sad news from home when he heard that his mother had also died.

Another member of the Forest of Dean group who certainly wrote home was Henry Shapcott. He had always pleaded innocence against the charge of rape and had raised several petitions before he was transported. On the 6th May 1859 he once again contacted the Colonial Office to ask that consideration be given for his early release. Henry reiterated that seven weeks had elapsed before he was charged with the crime of rape, during which time he had not tried to run away but had carried on with his lawful employment. The petition which landed on the desk of the Secretary of State for the Home Office in London referred to Henry's *'extreme youth at the time of conviction, his exemplary conduct since then, the long probation that he has now completed and the great amelioration which has been made in criminal code'.*[19] The Secretary of State was asked, *'to grant him a mitigation of sentence as early as convenient'*. On the 30th June 1859 the reply was received on board the *Medway* to say that Henry Shapcott had been unsuccessful and must continue with his sentence.

The days work for the convicts finished at 5 pm and after supper the men returned to their quarters to carry out any extra cleaning, including washing clothes. The chaplain who darted about in a fast sailing boat between each ship carried out evening prayers on board each hulk, and any hair cutting followed these and shaving that was required. When Anthony Trollope visited Boaz Island

The fortifications and dockyard on Ireland Island, Bermuda.
The Illustrated London News, 17th June 1848

Prison in 1859 he asked one of the prison officers '*and who shaves them?*' The unconcerned reply came back '*Oh, every man has his own razor, and they have knives too, though it is not allowed*'. It is not surprising that drunken brawls led to woundings and even murders on some occasions, as discipline by the officers was almost non-existent. After 8 pm the men were allowed time to themselves and it was now that they occupied their time by singing, drinking and fighting. After dark, much illicit trading was done with tobacco and rum. Some of the men read letters from home, over and over again and others carved models from pieces of the soft limestone. Eventually the men fell asleep in hammocks slung at arms length about a hundred or so together.

This recurring daily drudgery of hard work and hot humid conditions caused constant riots and bids for freedom. When rioting broke out among English and Irish convicts on board the *Medway* in 1859, the warders fled, closing the hatches and trapping the mutinous prisoners inside. During the brawl, an Englishman was killed and two Irish convicts stood trial for murder. Although the nearest mainland was some hundreds of miles away in the United States, convicts still tried their hand at escaping. They needed a boat and provisions and would terrorise the local population by threatening to murder them if they did not hand over the required food. Those who could not steal a boat often waited in the many caves around the island for the chance that a foreign vessel would pass near enough to pick them up and take them to safety. Severe punishment was levied on the prisoners when they were recaptured as John Mitchel reported after an attempted escape from the *Coromandel* in 1848. The men had seized a boat; but she had grounded on the reef and the men had to swim to shore. After hiding for a few days they were caught and sentenced to be flogged in each of the three hulks, a total of sixty lashes.

After the punishment Mitchel described what he had seen, an event which caused him much distress. '*The laceration is finished. The gangs are sent out to their work after being mustered to witness the example: the troops who were drawn up on the pier have marched home to their barracks: quarter-masters and guards have washed the blood-gouts from their arms and faces, and arranged their dress again: the three torn carcasses have been carried down half-dead to the several hospital rooms. Though shut up in my cell all the time, I heard the horrid screams of one man plainly. After being lashed in the* Medway, *they had all been carried to this ship, with blankets thrown over their bloody backs: and the first of them, after receiving a dozen blows with miserable shrieks, grew weak and swooned: the scourging stopped for about ten minutes while the surgeon used means to revive him – and then he had the remainder of his allowance. He was then carried groaning out of this ship into the* Coromandel, *instantly stripped again, and cross-scarified with another twenty lashes. The two other men took their punishment throughout in silence*'.

A large fire broke out in the dockyard in 1855, possibly started by a convict to cause damage. The fire soon became out of control and Richard Kear may well have been in the party who fought the blaze. Most of the convicts showed themselves at their best, carrying water from the sea to fill the fire engines and helping to direct the volumes of water onto the roofs. They succeeded in confining the flames to one large warehouse but even so the damage amounted to some £90,000, quite a sizeable sum as the Government were not insured for such a disaster. Some of the convicts took the opportunity to carry out wholesale looting and many who became hopelessly drunk on the proceeds then had to endure a flogging the next day.

Only the healthiest men were sent to Bermuda as the climate and heavy work required men to remain fit during their full term of imprisonment. There was no early release for good conduct and most convicts were kept to the last day of their sentence. If a convict did become ill and remained so for a period of twelve months he became a liability and was sometimes returned home. This meant that many of the men in their desperation to return home, even if only to another prison, would inflict terrible injuries and afflictions to themselves to gain admittance to hospital. William Sydes who was held prisoner on the *Coromandel* told of some of these ways. '*Some would grind glass to a powder and swallow it, so as to pass blood, others would make their own eyes so bad till they were near blinded and yet others would make bad legs by scratching the skin off the shin and applying tartar emetic to the wound mixed with salve which caused a very inflamed and ulcerated leg*'. Broken legs, ulcerated legs, bad eyes, and diarrhoea were the most prevalent complaints in Bermuda. It had to be a very strong man who could continue these awful punishments to himself for the full twelve months and although a few were invalided home, many were ruined for life.

There was, however, one disease that spared neither convict nor garrison and brought defence construction to a standstill so great was its devastation. Yellow Fever, known by the convicts as *Yellow Jack*, had visited Bermuda on several occasions but the worst epidemic occurred in the summer and autumn of 1853. The weather had been unusually wet and hot in July and August and the poorly ventilated hulks crowded with ill-fed and depressed men were the perfect breeding ground for the disease. Civilians too were caught up in the intensity of the outbreak with 85 deaths recorded amongst them. '*The defective sanitary conditions of the towns and the decomposing animal and vegetable matters on the shores of the numerous bays and creeks were considered important factors in the production of this epidemic*'.[20]

This particular outbreak had started brewing in the West Indies in the autumn of 1852, spreading along the coasts of the United States as far north as the Delaware River. In the spring of 1853, the *Blaseo de Garey* arrived at St. Georges from Havana where Yellow Fever was prevalent, bringing with her a disease of epidemic proportions. Several officers died on board the ship and the fever soon spread with devastating effect to the *Thames* convict hulk. One of the first fatal cases appeared on the 10th August 1853 on this hulk and '*by September*

12th, out of a total of 237 persons on board (the Thames *hulk) at the invasion of the disease, 194 were attacked and 57 were dead including 5 fatal cases among the guards of the ship'.*[21]

Many of the local people suffered constantly from diarrhoea and dysentery, probably caused by the poor water supply, but the first undoubted case of Yellow Fever among the native population occurred on the island of St. Davids where the pilot of the *Merlin* died on the 2nd August. At the other end of the Bermuda islands, Ireland Island was comparatively healthy and free of fever with the medical officer of the convict establishment only reporting a couple of incidences until cases from St. Georges began to arrive at the Royal Naval Hospital. William Sydes described this hospital, which was situated at the western end of Ireland Island, as a *'spacious beautiful building, three stories high with every possible comfort as a naval hospital'*. After 33 very bad cases were received at the hospital during September 1853, nurses and medical officers began to die and here too the local people contracted the disease. *'It fell with severity on one particular house, situated on the north shore at no great distance from the hospital privy then an open pit; it was occupied by the steward who contracted the disease and died in spite of the little intervention he had with the patients, his mother-in-law and brother-in-law both white natives living in the same house with him fell victims to the disease after his death'*.[22]

The *Bermuda Gazette* described the symptoms of the Yellow Fever in great detail, reporting that it was *'ushered in by langour and vigours, flushed face, a very severe and peculiar pain in the head, great uneasiness and pain in the back, loins and limbs, the eyes dull, glassy and suffused, the tongue furred and moist'*. They further commented, *'death sometimes occurs very unexpectedly even when the symptoms lead to the belief of recovery'*. Various doctors wrote to the newspaper offering potential cures. Dr Thomas Smith a Bermudan doctor living in New York sent a new prescription for the fever, which the *Gazette* reported, *'In the one instance in which it has been tried here it has proved successful'*. The treatment included taking a warm bath whilst at the same time having the head *"wet with cold water"'*. Next the patient was to be put to bed with hot bricks or bottles of hot water applied to the feet. *'After going to bed, have a large poultice made of finely cut tobacco and well moistened with molasses, applied to the stomach and bottoms of the feet; and also a poultice of grated onions covering the whole bowels'*. Dr. Smith also suggested giving a tea made from sage leaves and water together with *'a tea-spoonful of powdered loaf sugar containing one to two grains of mandrake'* this treatment to be continued until *'a copious perspiration is induced'*.

Yet another doctor who just signed himself as 'Quack' also suggested the sage leaf tea fortified with a little brandy but he stated that above all *'good nursing will carry a patient through when any medicine in the pharmacopoeia, prescribed by all the science of the most learned, has been tried and failed'*. This champion of the nursing profession ended his report by saying that *'many is the physician whose fame has been trumpetted forth as having cured an imagined incurable disease, but which in reality was effected by the nurse being at her post at the right moment'*. Although various treatments may have been carried out they had little effect and even though the commissioners immediately attended to the sanitary conditions within the dockyard it was too late and the death toll still rose.

The 56th regiment, stationed at the Casemates Barracks within the walls of the dockyard, suffered severely with 74 cases recorded out of a total of 440 men resulting in 22 deaths. All the soldiers of the 56th regiment who died both at Ireland Island and St. Georges are remembered on a memorial erected in St. Peters Church at St. Georges. Listed are Captain Hare and his wife, another captain and two lieutenants, the assistant surgeon Mr. Lawson, the bandmaster, 14 sergeants, 11 corporals, 2 drummers, 197 privates, 23 soldiers wives and 18 soldiers children. The list also includes Marion de Lisle the wife of Major Oakley and Albert William Dougherty the son of the quartermaster.

The convicts too, did not escape the *Yellow Jack* on board the hulks in Grassy Bay. The largest number of attacks occurred in the *Medway* and the least in the *Dromedary* whilst further outbreaks occurred at the Boaz Island Prison. All the convict cases were treated on board the hospital ship *Tenedos* and out of a total of 1,462 convicts, 468 were attacked and 92 men died.

The quarterly returns sent to England from the *Medway*, show that the men from the Forest of Dean suffered too, with only Richard Kear and George Charles being recorded as in good health in that September of 1853. James James and Henry Shapcott were shown as being sick, but the saddest remarks of all were given for Thomas James who died on the *Tenedos* on the 7th October and Hiram Archer who died on the 14th October.[23]

Thomas and Hiram would have been buried in the little graveyard on Watford Island, *'a bleak sandy spot, on its southern shore with patches of coarse grass scattered over it'*[24] surrounded by a wall and overlooking the sea. There are said to be over 400 convicts buried here but the size of the burial ground leads one to suspect that the ground was never consecrated. Convicts were just buried wherever there was a space in graves aligned north to south, as was the custom, so that the sun did not shine down straight on the bodies.

Simple headstones were erected to mark the passing of these unfortunate convicts, mostly only giving details of name and age. Inscriptions show how young many of these wretched men were, Thomas Jeffries aged 23 who died on the 2nd September 1853 *'Much respected by his officers and deeply regretted by his fellow prisoners'*, and Charles Dodd late quartermaster of Boaz Island Prisons who died 5th June 1854 aged 29 years, *'leaving a widow and five young children to lament their loss'*. One headstone erected in remembrance of Don Willis aged 27 who died on the 18th November 1853 has a poignant inscription which was most appropriate for all the men who lost their lives so far away from home.

'Farewell my friends, we meet no more;
No aid on earth my life could save;
For, banished from my native shore,
In foreign clime I found a grave'.[25]

Having survived harsh imprisonment in England, a rough sea crossing and a few months hard labour in Bermuda, Thomas James and Hiram Archer were sadly missed by their friends from the Forest of Dean.[26]

[1] Medway guns – 28 x 32 pounders, 28 x 18 pounders, 18 x 9 pounders. These guns were smoothbore muzzle-loaders firing round iron shot; the size of the gun listed being actually the weight of the shot.
[2] *The Andrew and the Onions* - Stranack p. 104
[3] *Convict Hulk Establishment* (Bermuda Historical Quarterly, Vol VIII) p. 123
[4] *Ibid*. p. 109
[5] PRO - Colonial Office Papers - CO 37/141: 28
[6] *Ibid*. - CO 37/147: 174
[7] *Convict Hulk Establishment* (Bermuda Historical Quarterly, Vol VIII) p. 152
[8] PRO - Colonial Office Papers - CO 37/175: 20
[9] *Ibid*. - CO 37/174: 253
[10] Bermuda Archives, Governors despatches CS 5/1/25 1851
[11] *Jail Journal* - Mitchel p. 63
[12] *Account of life on the convict hulks* - Sydes p. 32
[13] *Jail Journal* - Mitchel p. 98
[14] *Life Among Convicts* - Gibson pp. 44-47
[15] PRO - Colonial Office Papers - CO 37/175: 54
[16] *Bermuda's Convict Hulks* - Hollis-Hallett pp. 87-104
[17] *Ibid*. pp. 93-94
[18] PRO - Colonial Office Papers - CO 37/174: 127
[19] PRO - Home Office Papers - HO 18/833
[20] Bermuda Archives 81/1772 and 89/3389 *Epidemics of Yellow Fever at Bermuda 1853* - Harvey
[21] *Ibid*.
[22] *Ibid*.
[23] PRO - Home Office Papers - HO 8/118
[24] *The Bermuda Convict Establishment, 1863* - Mitchell p. 125
[25] *Ibid*.
[26] In May 1997 Alec and Averil Kear visited the little graveyard on Watford Island where they erected a small monument to Thomas James, not knowing at that time that Hiram Archer had also been buried there. Only three headstones were still in existence. One was for Thomas Jeffries aged 23 years who died 2.9.1853 stating 'Much respected by his officers and deeply regretted by his fellow prisoners'. The next was for John Taylor aged 28 years 'Expired of Yellow Fever on - November 1856'. The last stated 'Sacred to the memory of Charles H. Dodd late Quartermaster of Boaz Island prisons who died June 5th 1854 aged 29 yrs. Leaving a widow and 5 young children to lament their loss'.

Chapter Ten

HOME IS THE SAILOR

For the next eight years the four men worked hard at their tasks praying every day that some miracle might happen which would enable them to return to England's shores. They knew that they would have to see their term of imprisonment through, and perhaps all they could do was to hope for early release on the grounds of good behaviour even though they knew that this was improbable.

In 1855 the Cameronian Regiment commanded by Colonel Ferdinand Whittingham C.B. arrived from England on eighteen months' duty, and by this time convicts in Bermuda had been working on roads and fortifications for thirty years. Whittingham's main duties were to oversee the convicts on Ireland Island but he felt that this was a sordid job as *'No decent notion could germinate there'*.[1] He was particularly aggrieved when the British Army were commending themselves during the Crimean War whilst he was just *'watching convicts'*. His disinterested attitude meant that life aboard the hulks became as depraved as it could be with warders coping with mutinies and constant bids for freedom. Not all the convicts were notorious however, and in these the warders found allies. Some went to the aid of the warders when they were being attacked and there were nearly as many instances of warders saving convicts from drowning or from the wrath of their fellow prisoners.

During the eight years that Richard Kear, George Charles, James James and Henry Shapcott were held on board the *Medway* hulk their daily work would have involved them in the construction of many of the buildings at the dockyard which still survive today. Officers' houses were built in Dockyard Terrace, and houses in Victoria and Albert Row and Prince Alfred Terrace were constructed. By 1855 the great Victualling Yard had been completed, foundry and fitting shops were built in the North Yard and in 1859 a boat shed and engine house were erected in the Spar Yard. The hard stone used in these buildings was quarried from the Morrisby Plain behind the Casemates Prison and from within the dockyard itself and the convicts learnt how to cut and shape the huge blocks for the construction of the handsome pieces of architecture.

By 1860 there were 123 guns at the dockyard fortification, the largest number of any of the other forts on the islands. The Keep of the dockyard contained the Sea Service stores, which in 1857 housed a shell store and two bombproof magazines for 6,540 barrels of powder. Small boats were moored on the natural pool inside the Keep and were used to supply munitions to any fleet moored in Grassy Bay. The Keep was extremely secure with the only entrance to the sea being a small channel guarded by a portcullis.

Towards the end of the 1850s it became increasingly obvious that the days of the wooden sailing ship were numbered. New wooden ironclad steamships were being built together with iron-hulled, armour-plated warships. The guns of the dockyard defences had been eminently suitable for destroying wooden ships without receiving any damage to themselves, but these new strong fighting ships could withstand gunfire and inflict severe damage to the fortress artillerymen. Back in England, Lord Palmerston raised a Royal Commission to discuss the refurbishment of all naval fortifications at the main ports along the southern coasts of Britain.

A massive amount of £11,000,000 was to be spent and at the same time consideration was given to the upgrading of the most important overseas naval bases, particularly those at Halifax, Nova Scotia, Bermuda, Gibraltar and Malta. Although money was set aside for renewing the fortifications at Bermuda it was not until 1867 that work began to ensure that the thickest armour plate was installed and the heaviest guns that could be bought were put into place.

The Crimean War brought its own problems to Bermuda, as most of the soldiers required for the administration and guarding of the prisoners on Ireland Island were suddenly required to fight. When regiments returned to England after a term of duty at the dockyard they were not replaced and the number of personnel began to shrink significantly. Yellow Fever once again hit Bermuda in 1856. Not as badly as before but nevertheless, the number of deaths caused concern in England about the viability of spending large sums of money sending convicts out to Bermuda, only to find that they were struck down by this virulent disease. Warders on the hulks were becoming increasingly tired of the constant fighting which broke out on board. One comptroller's annual report in 1859 alludes to '*a deplorable outburst of national excitement and animosity between the English and Irish prisoners. This animosity led to several fights, in one of which on 1st June last, a convict was unfortunately killed*'.[2]

Originally transportation had seemed an excellent way to rid the United Kingdom of its criminal population but it became apparent that the deterrence of transportation was not a severe enough punishment. People in England ignored the stories from released prisoners of the extreme suffering inflicted on the convicts, hearing only about easier times and plentiful food in far off countries. After Jebb reported that home imprisonment cost less than had been expected, and, as English gaols were not full it was decided to consider the abolition of transportation as a means to reform the criminal.[3]

In 1861 Mr. Childers in the House of Commons in London proposed that a select committee be asked to inquire into the present state of transportation. He commented '*we are now spending for purposes of penal discipline no less than*

£640,000 a year, of which £400,000 is expended upon establishments at home, and £200,000 upon those abroad'. His report went on to say that in Western Australia, Bermuda and Gibraltar there were now only 3,700 convicts and during the year of 1860 only 269 criminals had been transported. Transportation to Tasmania and New South Wales had been abandoned in 1852. Prisons, which had been built in England during the 1850s on the assumption that a certain proportion of criminals would be transported, were still found to have sufficient room to receive convicts. The average number of people imprisoned in England and Wales during the three years preceding 1861 had dropped from around 25,000 to 18,000 and Mr. Childers felt that the time had now come to abolish the unnecessary expense of transportation.[4]

The War Office and the Admiralty still wanted to use convict labour as a cheap means of building and maintaining their establishments throughout the world. Western Australia were still prepared to receive convicts not so much for the labour they provided as the large government subsidy of around $160,000 a year that went with it. Other Australian colonies, however, pointed out that on the arrival of the convicts, the free settlers left. Released prisoners were given conditional pardons, which meant that they could never return home but could move into neighbouring colonies. In one year in Victoria, conditionally pardoned men committed three-quarters of all crime. A Royal Commission on transportation in 1863 recommended that transportation as a deterrent be continued but the government had by now made up its mind that a more structured approach to imprisonment was required. In 1865 Parliament passed the Prison Act which stated that in 1867 all transportation would cease.

All the vast projects at the dockyard on Ireland Island were nearing completion, and consequently, by 1861 it was decided not to send any more convicts to Bermuda. Mr. Childer's report highlighted the fact that on economical grounds the present system of transportation to Bermuda required consideration. *'The annual cost of every convict there was £44, the proportion of sick was very large, and there was no proper supervision of the convict work, the amount of which was utterly incommensurate both with their number and the object for which they were sent thither'*.

It had always been intended that the convicts should be housed in the Boaz Barracks, which opened in 1848, but the hulks had not been abandoned then and the convicts had to endure many more years of depravity, and sweltering stinking conditions on board. The decision to close the convict establishment meant the abandonment of the hulks could now be put into action and the men were removed to Boaz Island to await their return to England. Some prisoners with terms of imprisonment nearly over knew that freedom would await them on their return whilst others faced an uncertain future in English prisons.

Some convicts who had committed crimes whilst in Bermuda had been sentenced to extra terms of imprisonment on board the hulks. The abolition of the establishment meant that these men could no longer be held in Bermuda

Commissariat, Bermuda,
HAMILTON, 17TH JUNE, 1861.

TENDERS, in Duplicate, will be received at
This Office, until Noon of

SATURDAY,

The 10th August, 1861,

FOR THE CHARTER OF A VESSEL
TO CONVEY ABOUT 200
CONVICTS,
To the United Kingdom,
VIZ.:—

To Spike Island in Ireland, and to
Portsmouth in England.

Accommodation will be required for such Officers
in the Cabin or Steerage as may be ordered to embark as Escort to the Convicts, and for any Officers,
Women or Children of the Convict Department
(the number of Adult Passengers not to exceed
six) who may be ordered a passage, either in the
Cabin or Steerage, including a suitable Mess, at the
Owner's expense. The Vessel must be ready to
Sail *on or about 1st September Next,* and should
commence fitting immediately after the Notification
of the acceptance of the Tender.

The space between decks must not be less than
5 feet 10 inches from deck to beam overhead. The
space for Hammocks not less than 14 inches apart,
and the space for each Convict embarked not less
than 9 feet 2 inches by 14 inches.

The Vessel must be provided with suitable iron
water, and stream Anchors and Cables, in good Condition,
and with all proper Sails, (not less than two Mainsails, two Maintopsails, and two Foresails, and two
Foretopsails,) and with a complete Set of Small
Sails—also with three good sized Boats, gratings to
hatchways, Water Closets for Men and Passengers,
&c., &c. She must likewise be fitted with Coppers
or furnaces, as well as with Coal or Wood for the
boiling or dressing of Provisions, for 200 Convicts;
also with cans and pumps for fresh water for said
Convicts on the voyage, as well as with measures,
weights, and scales legally stamped. She must be
provided with a spare Maintopsail Yard and another
Rough Spar, capable of being made into a jib-boom
or Maintopmast, and be otherwise properly equipped, fitted and furnished with Masts, Yards, Anchors, Ropes, Cords, Tackel, Apparel, Furniture, and
all other Articles and things necessary, proper, convenient, and fitting for such a Ship on her intended
Voyage. The whole at the expense of the Owners.

The necessary materials for the fittings to be
furnished by the Owner and put up by the Government. Provisions for Seven Weeks for the
Convicts will be put on board by Government,
and a proper Account of their issue must be rendered by the Master of the vessel, together with Receipts from the proper Officer of the Victualling
Department in England for the remains of Provisions and Stores before the freight will be paid.

The Tender to specify the terms of Charter in a
block Sum, and it is to be understood that no
Tender will be accepted unless the terms are approved and the vessel is found suitable in every respect
for the Service, according to the decision of the
Surveying Officers appointed by Government.

The Vessel will be Surveyed at Government expense.

Two responsible Sureties, whose Original Signatures must be affixed on the face of the Tender, and
who will be held jointly and severally bound to Her
Majesty the Queen in the penal sum of Five Hundred Pounds Sterling each, of the lawful Money of
Great Britain, will be required for the due and
faithful performance of the Charter party.

Payment will be made in Treasury Bills at Par
by this Department on the completion of the Service
and the production of a Certificate from the Officer
in Charge of the Convict Department at Boaz Island, that the Service has been duly completed, and
the Stores satisfactorily accounted for.

Any further information may be obtained on application to This Office.

L. ROUTH,
Dy.-Comy.-Genl.

SALE OF

MEDWAY,

Late Convict Hulk.

THE MEDWAY, late Convict Hulk, having been
directed to be Sold for the purpose of being
broken up; Tenders, in Duplicate, will be received
at My Office until

Thursday, the 15th June,
Next, At Noon,

For the Purchase of that HULK,

As she now lies along-side the Dock Yard Wharf,
with the exception of her ballast.

The Tenders to state the price which will be
given on two separate conditions, either of which
may be adopted by Government, Vizt.:—

1st. That the Old Copper and mixed Metal, only,
arising from the Hulk, shall be returned into my
charge, at the present Government rates for those
articles; and 2nd, that the offal Wood or Firewood,
in addition to the Copper and mixed Metal, shall
likewise be returned, to be paid for by Government
at the rate of 12s. 6d. per cord, and taken from the
purchaser's hands at the Public expense.

The following are the principal additional conditions of Sale.

The Hulk to be removed from the Dock Yard
as soon after the acceptance of the Tender as may
be required, and such removal to be at the risk of
the Purchaser; but the Government will furnish a
temporary rudder (to be returned) and give the
assistance of a Steamer, without charge, to transport the Vessel to any point in these Islands to
which the purchaser may wish to have her taken
and whither she can be floated, and will also lend such
anchors and chain cables as may be necessary for
her security there, the purchaser being liable for
any damages or deficiencies which may be found on
the return of the Stores so lent.

The price to be paid in three instalments; the
first immediately after the agreement is signed; the
second 6 months thereafter, and the third within 12
months after the date of the agreement.

Two responsible persons will be required to join
with the purchaser as Sureties to Government in
the sum of £500 for the due fulfilment of the agreement on his part.

Further particulars may be obtained at My Office,
and the Hulk inspected at any time during the
working hours of the Yard.

JOHN MARTIN,
Naval Storekeeper.

Bermuda Yard,
26th May, 1865.

*An advertisement for vessels to charter for
bringing prisoners back to the United
Kingdom, taken from the Bermuda Royal
Gazette of 17th June 1861.*
courtesy Chris Addams

The sale of the Medway *in 1865 as announced in
the Bermuda Royal Gazette.*
courtesy Chris Addams

and '*several rascals thus escaped with comparative immunity for their Bermuda crimes*'.[5]

Although many warders and government workers of the convict establishment remained on the island, only one convict was ever allowed to stay. William Facey had been an exemplary prisoner and when his term of imprisonment was over he was released on the island with no questions asked. He went on to become the first liveryman on Bermuda and ran a successful mail service. He prospered and took on a new business breeding hogs. '*He grew the largest hogs in the colony and once put them on view for 6d a look*'.[6]

Richard Kear, George Charles, James James and Henry Shapcott were removed from the *Medway* at the beginning of 1861 to await their return to England. The quarterly / half yearly prison returns from the *Medway*, for prisoner No.2047, James James, show that his behaviour deteriorated over the years with 8 quarters of 'very good', 22 of 'good' and 2 of 'indifferent'. He was transferred to Boaz Island on the 13th February 1861, and here the records show one more quarter of 'very bad' behaviour.[7] At the time of his return in 1862, his behaviour was noted as 'good' and he was stated to be 'healthy'. Both Richard Kear and George Charles were noted as having 'very good' and 'good' behaviour for the whole term of their imprisonment. Henry Shapcott, still pleading his innocence, was not discharged from Bermuda until the 23rd January 1862.

The *Bermuda Gazette* asked for tenders to be received for the charter of vessels to convey convicts to the United Kingdom. Specific accommodation was required on these ships for officers escorting the prisoners and any women and children of the convict department who were returning home. One advertisement in June 1861 gave the measurements required on board. '*The space between the decks must not be less than 5 feet 10 inches from deck to beam overhead. The spaces for hammocks not less than 14 inches apart and the space for each convict embarked not less than 9 feet 2 inches by 14 inches*'. There were to be water closets for men and passengers and '*she must likewise be fitted with coppers or furnaces, as well as with coal or wood for the boiling or dressing of provisions, for 200 convicts, also with cans and pumps for fresh water for said convicts*'. Provisions for the seven-week voyage were to be put aboard by the victualling stores in Bermuda. No money would be paid over to the owner of the ship unless a proper account was kept of the issue of the food and a receipt obtained from the Officer of the Victualling Department in England for the remains of the provisions and stores. Too many convicts had starved on voyages in the past at the expense of well-fed officers.

The ship chartered to take Richard Kear home was the *Sir George Seymour*. Thomas Davis and Joseph John Outerbridge of Shelly Bay in Bermuda had built her in 1853. She was a barque of 267 tons with beautiful lines and had been built for speed. On one occasion, with a full load of convicts on board, she went to Queenstown, Ireland, in twelve and a half days, and once made a return trip from Land's End in nineteen days. Her owners[8] were justifiably proud of

The Sir George Seymour.   National Maritime Museum

her and entered her for the transatlantic race from Sandy Hook to the Needles for a $90,000 prize. The *Henrietta* beat her and the Bermudians were not impressed. However, when they eventually saw the *Henrietta* with all sail set they had to acknowledge that she was a wonder to behold.

The *Sir George Seymour* was taken over by Thomas Melville Dill and Thomas Newbold, with Dill becoming the master responsible for transporting convicts from Bermuda to London. In April 1863 the *Sir George Seymour* was chartered to return the last 136 convicts to England. Her master at that time was Captain J. H. Watlington and the convicts were in the care of Dr. C. F. Edwards. W. E. Adderley, a cabin boy on board the *Sir George Seymour*, used to tell this story '*Capt. Watlington went to church on Sunday mornings when in port, dressed in immaculate white. One June Sunday in the Thames, Adderley was at the gangway for the Captain – but he touched the ladder slightly with his oar*'. There was only one more sentence to this story: '*That man's hand was as large as a ham*'. [9]

The *Sir George Seymour* arrived at Bermuda on the 25th March 1861, ready to take another consignment of convicts back to England. On the the 10th April 1861 Richard Kear and George Charles took their last look at the dockyard, the Boaz Island Prison and the shores of Bermuda and set sail for home. James James and Henry Shapcott were discharged from Boaz Island in the spring of 1862.

A small tug towed the *Sir George Seymour* out to sea from the Camber at

Ireland Island and she then set sail on the ocean alone. The Medical Officer was as usual given instructions concerning the convicts in his charge. Many would have been invalid patients from the hospital at Boaz Island and yet others had various diseases for which it was necessary to provide the requisite care and medical attention. As on the journey out all those years ago, many of the convicts succumbed to seasickness until they found their sea legs and some suffered for the whole voyage.

The first stop on her voyage home that April in 1861 was San Juan in Puerto Rico. This may have been to take passengers on board or to collect a cargo of sugar and rum for England. Once fully laden the convicts on the *Sir George Seymour* settled down to surviving the voyage to England. Theodore Godet M.D., Medical Officer in charge of the *Devonshire* kept a diary on the voyage from Bermuda to the United Kingdom in 1859. His portrayal of life aboard during that trip must have been repeated many times on other convict transports. He spoke of the schemers who tried to instil his sympathy by feigning illness, in order to obtain a 'crapper' of rum. Godet's answer was to give a 'crapper' of saltwater, which usually caused a miraculous recovery. He described the 'Dog Watch' between 6-8 pm when prisoners not suffering from illness were allowed to enjoy themselves as they pleased although still under the watch of an officer. At 8 o'clock the officer on guard would order all prisoners below decks and *'order and stillness were enforced'*. [10]

Godet went on to describe mealtimes and spoke of the pleasure when the mate caught a four foot long porpoise which was served up as a welcome change to the salt provisions. On his voyage on the *Devonshire* there was a black cook, who although nearly always drunk, showed a little compassion by taking care of a tabby cat and two kittens. He was always able to provide special and very tasty pies for the Captain and the cabin passengers and Godet wondered how he managed to find fresh meat, which was always in short supply. Godet's diary says *'on one occasion I discerned part of a Rat and the claw of a Kitten in the neighbourhood of the cooking apparatus'*. At first the black cook denied using anything other than meat supplied but when pressed further he said *'Dis boy does him best at all times – and Captain always wants weal Pies – and me gib weal Pies as long as Kittens last. When Kittens is out, den me get um Rats – and very fine Rats dey are too – dem very fat and sweet – um make nice Pies and Ragouts'*. [11]

For the next few weeks Richard Kear and George Charles endured the cramped conditions and the rolling of the ship. The Captain and crew of these convict transports often had to show great judgement and nautical skill whilst riding out a severe gale. Most ships reached their destination safely but the story of the *Cedrine* was recounted for many years. She was a new clipper of 308 tons when in 1862 she was chartered for a voyage from Bermuda to Portsmouth. She had on board 189 English prisoners and two Irish. All went well on the trip until a thick fog descended near the Isle of Wight. The Captain, Thomas Dill, was a very able seaman and was not worried at this stage as he changed course for Portsmouth. At midnight Dill turned the ship over to the mate and headed for his bed. Just after 1 am the *Cedrine* passed the Eddystone light but soon after the mate mistook a red light for that of a vessel going down the channel *'and at 1.40 am, with a brimming tide, the* Cedrine *went fast upon a rock'.* [12]

Coast guards managed to get everyone on shore by about 4 am and most of the convicts went straight to the nearby public houses where several of them produced enough cash, one up to £23, for the majority to get very drunk. All the prisoners had supposedly been searched before boarding the steam tug *Siren*, which took them out to the *Cedrine* on leaving Bermuda; consequently the funds in the hands of the convicts posed a problem. Either the money had been secretly stored away by the prisoners or more likely the local labourers who often worked alongside the convicts had held it. At any rate the men were soon rounded up and taken on to Millbank Prison to be properly discharged but the whole episode showed the complete breakdown of Bermudan authority over the prisoners. Captain Dill lost his master's ticket and the mate's account of the shipwreck was most unsatisfactory, as it would appear that he had been too tired to take on his duties that night.

Eventually, on the 11th June 1861, the convicts on board the *Sir George Seymour* saw the shores of England. A sight that most never dreamt they would ever see again. The ship dropped anchor at Falmouth for the night and then continued round the coast arriving in London at Millbank on the following day. After disembarking some of the convicts she then continued her voyage to Deal on the Kentish coast, arriving on the 18th June. On the same day she continued to Gravesend where the last convicts were put ashore for the short journey to Chatham Prison. It was here that Richard Kear and George Charles once more set foot on England's shores. Even though their term of imprisonment was not over the sights and sounds of England on that short trip to Chatham must have gladdened their hearts.

The hardest part of their imprisonment was still to come, however, as conditions in Chatham Prison were most appalling.

Chatham Prison had been built in 1856 based on the model penitentiary at Pentonville. It was another in a number of prisons designed to replace the system of transportation with penal servitude at home. The convicts at Chatham were employed at St Mary's Island in building an addition to the old naval dockyard so once again the Forest of Dean men found themselves heaving and cutting rock and shovelling mud. Only this time conditions were harsh and the weather not so kind as in Bermuda. The site of the works at Chatham covered around 430 acres and the whole area was drained and surrounded by a sea wall nearly two miles in length. All the work was carried out by convict labour and the men would have been employed in excavating, pile-driving and concreting, for the foundations; brick-laying, concreting, stone-dressing and setting, in connection with the construction of the basin walls and entrances; removing

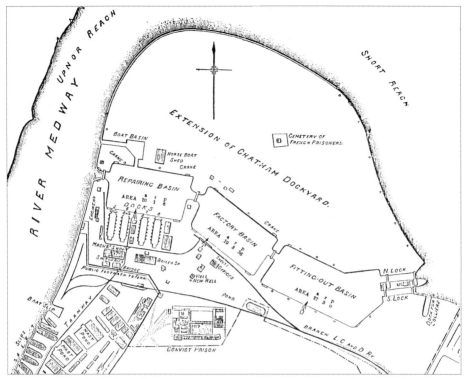

St Mary's Island, Chatham showing the convict prison.   courtesy Rochester Public Library

the earth from the area of the basin by means of waggons and incline planes, barrow roads, barrow lifts, and tipping waggons; loading and unloading materials; plate-laying; and attending standing and locomotive engines.[13] The scheme was vast and it was alleged that these mud filled basins *'were places where more human blood was spilt and more human lives lost through excessive labour than in any other prison'.*[14]

George Bidwell had been a prisoner at Chatham in the 1870s and he told of the extreme hardship of the convicts during their working day. He spoke of the never-ending drudgery of loading trucks with clay, which was then taken to the giant pug-mill.[15] The trucks held four tons of clay and there were three men to a truck, and they were expected to fill nineteen trucks a day. These trucks had to be run up planks of no more than eight inches wide on a very steep slope before being emptied into the pug mill. Bidwell described how frightened the convicts were of the punishment they would receive if the work was not accomplished, he said, *'it was despairing work'*.

The cellblocks that housed Richard Kear and George Charles were in the form of an inverted T, with an exercise yard on either side. Tiers of cells looked down on a central hall. Each individual cell had a small window, a door with

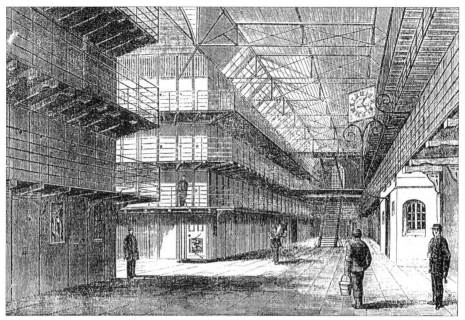

Interior of St. Mary's Convict Prison, Chatham.
The Illustrated London News, 9th March 1861.

an eyehole, and floors of asphalt. Many had thin corrugated iron walls making communication between the men extremely easy. A small knock on the wall announced the arrival of a warder in the corridor and at this point talking ceased until he had passed by.

The strict regime at Chatham started with the first bell at 5.30 am calling the convicts to wash themselves usually in a large stone trough of cold water. Cell cleaning came next, including the portion of landing outside the cell door and when breakfast was finished plates had to be cleaned and beds made.

The diet in Chatham Prison was of the worst kind consisting mostly of black bread and potatoes with about six ounces of meat per day. They were sometimes given a watery soup and they were allowed one pint of tea with sugar and milk on four days a week and on the other three the tea was substituted by one pint of cocoa. Supper was always one pint of gruel.[16] Richard Kear and George Charles had received reasonable food in Bermuda and had arrived back in England sunburnt and healthy. On such a meagre diet with such excessive hard work expected of them, many of the convicts soon began to waste away and became so desperate for food that they often resorted to eating grass, candles and even earth.

Their minds became affected too and this deep despair pushed many of them into trying to end their miserable lives, or at least to send them to the comparative ease of the hospital. A favourite way at Chatham to inflict an injury was provided by the wagons in which the clay was moved around. A convict would run from his working party and deliberately lay his legs on the rails in front of the oncoming trucks. Another way to escape the agony of the arduous work expected was shown by the convicts who would rather undergo dietary punishment than dig another clod of clay. They would throw down the spade and turn their backs on the warder saying that they did not intend to work any more that day. They allowed their hands to be handcuffed thus effectively taking them out of the workplace and there they remained until it was time to be marched back to their cells. This was, of course, not popular with the other men, who had to make good the work.

Every morning at 7 am, before turning out for work, warders and convicts alike went to chapel. It was one of the few times when the men could talk to each other and usually the service was an uproar of swearing and shouting.

After chapel the working parties were assembled in the yard and meticulously searched, the object being to guard against any tools or food being taken out which might be used in an escape attempt. Sometimes the whole gang would be marched off to the bathhouse to be strip searched whilst the cells of each convict were turned upside down for any hidden items.

The actual dockyard extension at Chatham was started around 1864 and so Richard Kear and George Charles who arrived in 1861 would have been set to work on building the embankment, which was to protect St. Mary's Island from the tidal Medway. This embankment was faced with stone and was built high enough to stop the highest spring tide. Working conditions were wet and laborious and prison officers enforced very severe discipline. Many men were unused to hard labour and one of the few major disturbances in a nineteenth century prison broke out at Chatham in February 1861, just before Richard and

The parade ground at St. Mary's Convict Prison, Chatham.
The Illustrated London News, 2nd March 1861.

George arrived. The convicts smashed furniture and fittings in the mess house on St. Mary's Island and the Governor was forced to call on military help to stop the affair. Another similar mutiny took place a few days later and over £1,000 of property was destroyed during the two incidents.

Prison warders were certainly not the moral reformers needed for the job. In the first four years from the opening of the prison in 1856, 54 warders resigned their duty out of which 16 were dismissed for drunkenness.[17] They were often heard exchanging obscenities with the prisoners and George Bidwell heard one assistant warder reflect that his fellow warders were mostly '*too much of a coward to steal, ashamed to beg, too lazy to work*' and therefore became a soldier then a prison warder.[18]

The men who survived best under this harsh regime were those who went along without protest. Richard Kear and George Charles knew that they were within a year or two of release. Their past prison record had shown them having good conduct and they may well have been placed in a gang of special convicts trusted to work alone and unguarded in repayment for good behaviour.

Around noon the convicts were marched back to their cells for lunch, such as it was, and a rest of about 1 hour. They were searched again and sent back to work by 1.30 pm and the day finished at around 5 pm when the desperately tired men dragged themselves back to the last meal of the day and the prospect of being shut up for about twelve hours on their own.

It was August 1863 when Richard Kear and George Charles were summoned to the Governor's office.[19] They had known for some time that their release was imminent. They had been allowed to grow their hair a little longer and they had both been measured up for a rough suit of clothing and boots. The two men were informed that they would be released just two or three days after completing 12 years of imprisonment but they would be subject to 'ticket-of-leave' conditions. This meant that they would have to report to their nearest police station once a month and if they did not do so then it could mean many more years in prison. Despite this warning, many prisoners did not keep to these conditions. Gaining work at home was impossible if a man had to explain to an employer that he was just out of prison. The police too, did not seek out these men as long as they knew the released convict was in employment and not committing any crimes.

During the whole term of their imprisonment convicts were paid 3d. per day as wages. Two pence of this had to be paid over for board and lodging and the rest was kept by the government to be given to the prisoner on his release. In 1857 the Discharged Prisoners' Aid Society was established. This Society dealt only with convicts released from government prisons who were going to live and work in London. The Society held all the prisoners' entitlement of money and gave it back to the men in small amounts to save it being squandered all in one go at the nearest hostelry. Needless to say, at the beginning the Society did not have a good reputation as most of the funds seemed to end up in the

St. Mary's Island, convicts at work.   The Illustrated London News, 9th March 1861.

pockets of the administrators. Similar charitable organisations were formed in other localities and as Richard and George were not intending to stay in London their money may have been sent to a Gloucester charity organisation. The money they had accrued over the twelve years, amounted to around £18 each, not a large amount for the years of pain and hardship they had endured.

Richard and George heard the Governor's voice telling them that they were now free to go and as they followed the warder to the gate the effort to control the desire to scream and shout with happiness must have been unbearable. As the gate swung open on that August day they surely felt like Michael Davitt *'that the punishment involved in a penal servitude of that duration would be worth enduring again to enjoy the wild, ecstatic, soul-filling happiness of the first day of freedom'.*[20]

They would at first have been bewildered by the hustle and bustle of the streets as they made their way to the railway station to board a train for London. Their days had been so structured that the decisions they now had to make for themselves undermined their confidence and made them nervous. They had been given a railway ticket to take them from Chatham to London and a small amount of money to use after that. The train journey through the Kentish countryside showed them what they had been missing for the last twelve years. Orchards of apple trees stood side by side with fields of wheat and yet others where sleek well-fed cows grazed happily. As the train drew into London they would have been amazed at the changes which had taken place since they left

Millbank all those years before. Everybody and everything was in a hurry and there were many more trains at the London terminus all heaving and snorting. They had been told what to do on arrival at London and as soon as they had bought their tickets they boarded the train to take them to Gloucester.

Now and only now did their feelings overwhelm them and apprehension about their homecoming took over. Would they be accepted back into the community and how would their families react to seeing them again? Richard Kear must have wondered about his wife Charlotte and daughter Phoebe who would by now be 12 years old. All of these thoughts were pushed to one side as the familiar landscape of Gloucestershire began to unfold and they realised that after all that had happened to them they were at last GOING HOME.

[1] *Bermuda from sail to steam* - Wilkinson p. 659
[2] Annual report on the convict establishments at Bermuda & Gibraltar. (Printed by George Eyre & William Spottiswoode HMSO 1858-1862)
[3] *Convicts and the Colonies* - Shaw p. 357
[4] Bermuda Gazette 1.3.1861
[5] Bermuda Journal of Archaeology and Maritime History Vol 9 p. 126
[6] *Bermuda from Sail to Steam* - Wilkinson
[7] PRO HO8/148 Prison returns
[8] Original owners of the *Sir George Seymour – Bermuda from sail to steam* p. 654
N. T. Butterfield (18 shares)
N. A. Butterfield (8 shares)
J. H. Trimingham (18 shares)
Henry Mills Stowe Capt; (4 shares)
The builders (8 shares)
[9] *Bermuda from Sail to Steam* - Wilkinson p. 654
[10] *The Forty Thieves* - Goder p. 82
[11] *Ibid.* p. 87
[12] *Bermuda from Sail to Steam* - Wilkinson p. 677
[13] *Account of the manner in which Sentences of Penal Servitude are carried out in England* - DuCane
[14] *Victorian Prison Lives* - Priestley p. 132
[15] Pug Mill = Clay mixed with water in a pug mill to form a malleable mass or paste for making bricks and pottery. (Oxford English Dictionary).
[16] *Criminal Ancestors* - Hawkings p. 22
[17] *Victorian Prison Lives* - Priestley p. 255
[18] *Ibid.*
[19] Chatham Convict Prison, Officers, 1862
Governor Capt. Folliott Powell,*Deputy Governor* Major Ogelvie, *Chief Medical Officer* J. J. D. Burns RN, *Assistant Surgeon* John Smith, *Chaplain* Rev. John K. Marsh, MA, *Assistant Chaplain* Rev. J. B. Duke, *Steward* Robert Bruce, *Chief Warder* Edwin Kinch (Kelly's Directory of Kent 1862)
[20] *Leaves from a prison diary Vol II* - Davitt p. 168

Chapter Eleven

OTHER ROADS TO FREEDOM

Henry Shapcott and James James watched longingly as their two friends boarded the *Sir George Seymour*, which was to return them to England, but it was not their turn to return home until the beginning of 1862. The two of them left the Boaz Island prison in Bermuda and arrived at Portsmouth Prison on the 5th April 1862.

Henry SHAPCOTT

As soon as Henry Shapcott arrived at Portsmouth he lost no time in raising yet another petition which he sent to the Home Office on the 23rd May 1862.[1] Once again he pleaded his innocence, stressing as before that he had witnesses to prove that he was at home when the crime was committed all those years ago in 1851. The petition went on to say that none of these witnesses had been called to give evidence on his behalf even though they had travelled some 15 miles to attend the hearing. Henry pointed out that his behaviour in Millbank and Bermuda had been 'good' and that others convicted for similar crimes had been given shorter sentences. As before, the petition ended with a plea that his case be 'mercifully' considered. The Secretary of State decided that it was too soon for his discharge, especially as no one had stated what his employment would be on his release. The chaplain at Portsmouth Prison said that Henry Shapcott would get his living as a miner but could not say who his employer would be. The decision of the Home Office was that a further petition should be raised in March 1863 when this information might be forthcoming. Meanwhile, Henry Shapcott, number 7127, remained in prison.

There was already a borough gaol in Portsmouth and when in 1850 work started on building an additional prison to house convicts awaiting transportation the plan was not popular. A petition to the Queen spoke of the fears of local residents in having villains in such close proximity to the housing next to the dockyard. Although the residents would have preferred the prisoners to stay on board the prison ships, the convicts themselves must have been only too pleased to leave the dark damp hulks, which had been a familiar sight in Portsmouth harbour since the 1780s.

The prison was based on the same plan as Portland and contained 1,000 separate sleeping-cells.[2] It was a four-storey building with an infirmary and a chapel. Convicts worked as labourers in the dockyard and on other government works as required. A convict writing home to his brother in 1866 after he had been held in Portsmouth Prison spoke of *'dragging about wood or iron, cleaning the sides of vessels, cleaning out docks and coaling'*. This same man wrote of the living conditions in the prison. He told of the cells like iron boxes 7ft. by 4ft. and just over 6ft. high *'in which you have everything to do in almost perfect darkness, and which is so ill provided with vessels and other means of cleanliness that to get through your cell cleaning at all is like working a Chinese puzzle'.*[3]

Those men serving long-term sentences came to school in the chapel for half a day per week. One hundred men at a time were taught the basic rudiments of reading, writing and geography.[4] Once again this new prison was designed to introduce a more stringent routine for criminals whilst endeavouring to morally reform them.

Discipline was harsh but most of the inmates were hardened criminals. A doctor who carried out a term of duty at Portsmouth spoke of being *'suddenly transplanted into a veritable community of pirates capable of any, and every, crime under the sun'.*[5] Even though penalties for misconduct were severe they appeared to have little effect and the only inducement to good behaviour was the promise of an earlier release date.

On the 20th November 1863 the offices at Whitehall again reconsidered the possible release of Henry Shapcott. This time the petition gave much more information. Henry's father was named as T. Shapcott of Drybrook near Mitcheldean and Rev. Nicholls, the minister of Holy Trinity at Drybrook stated *'I am truly happy to be able to report most satisfactorily as to his friends and prospects Mr. Brain will assuredly put him to work'*. The comment on the bottom of this petition notes *'To be again submitted for the Secretary of States consideration in the Month of March 1864'.*[6] Henry must have been in despair by now wondering if he was ever to be released.

Shortly after George Charles and Richard Kear returned home, they visited the parents of Henry Shapcott to talk about their long ordeal. Henry's parents were amazed that their son was still being held prisoner when these two men had been released and they immediately wrote to Henry asking that he make a further representation to the Secretary of State.

On the 2nd April 1864 Henry Shapcott raised yet another petition which read as follows:

'Your petitioner was tried for rape at Gloucester in 1852 and was sentenced to transportation for life. I have completed over twelve years and have been a well-conducted man. In the same case with your petitioner were six others, five were tried in August 1851. Three were sentenced to transportation for life and two fifteen years. One was tried with your petitioner and was also sentenced to transportation for life and has since died. I wish to draw your attention to the fact that out of seven men tried for the same offence your petitioner is the only one still in prison. One sentenced for life and one for fifteen years having died. The other fifteen years man was liberated in 1859. Another sentenced for life went to Australia. The other two sentenced for life were liberated from Chatham in last August. Their names were Kear and Charles. I know this by a letter that I received from my parents who had been called upon by one of these men.

That your petitioner has been longer in prison than Kear and Charles who were liberated two or three days after they had completed twelve years. My conduct during imprisonment has been equally as good as theirs. I was never in prison before. I have been upwards of twelve years in prison. And I humbly beg and beseech you to shew me the same clemency that was displayed to those in the same case. And thereby gladden the sorrowing hearts of my parents, relatives and friends'.

The Secretary of State replied to the director at Portsmouth Prison '*If he has undergone now as long a term as the others had when released then he may have a licence, if not then held back until he has*'.[7]

In August 1864 Henry Shapcott at last walked to freedom

James JAMES

After returning from Bermuda, prisoner No. 7120 James James was only held in Portsmouth Prison for four months. His conduct whilst on board the *Medway* in Bermuda was noted as 'very bad' and he would have undoubtedly finished his sentence there but for the fact that the last of the Bermuda hulks were deactivated in 1862. On the 23rd September 1862, 80 men were brought from Chatham and put on board the *York*, a convict ship bound for Australia. On the 3rd October the ship called at Portland and picked up James James and 133 other convicts who were to sail with him to the other side of the world.

This voyage of the *York* was the twenty-sixth shipment of convicts to Western Australia. Besides the 213 convicts, there were on board 104 guards and their families and four other cabin passengers. The captain on the voyage was C. Breacey and the surgeon responsible for the overall well being of everyone was Mr. Babington.

James James knew that he would never return home but by 1862 when he set sail he had heard of convicts being released in this new country and making a comfortable living for themselves.

A transport ship was practically in the hands of the men she was carrying once she had set sail, and most of the crew knew by long experience that it was best to leave these ruffians to their own devices to ensure a safe, quiet voyage. The prisoners on board the *York* were no exception to this and during the voyage to Western Australia the men were left to lounge about, read and talk and smoke (above deck) as they pleased, '*obliged only to keep their part of the ship clean, and do what is necessary for health and cleanliness*'.[10]

Convicts on this voyage felt a sense of freedom and singing and dancing were regular occurrences. Some of the men even made a little money on the voyage if they were prepared to work as a servant for one of the wealthier prisoners. Compared with the meals in Portsmouth Prison of mutton and vegetable stew, the rations on board the *York* were good, *'good pork, good pease-soup and good plum-dough'*.[11] There were inevitably a few fights on the voyage especially after the men were put on salt rations about halfway through the journey but again the master of the ship left the men to sort out their own quarrels to keep the peace on board.

The master of the *York*, Captain Breacey took control of his ship and after a very speedy voyage lasting just 84 days reached Freemantle on the 31st December 1862.[12] The surgeon was pleased to report that there had only been one death on the voyage, that of prisoner number 6701, Henry Payne.

Around 1826, a young navy captain, James Stirling, had a vision that the Swan River area in Western Australia would be worth developing. With the help of Thomas Peel, an English landowner, the requisite funds were raised and a company formed called Thomas Peel & Co. The Colonial Office gave the company 250,000 acres on the Swan with a promise of a further 250,000 acres after 400 settlers had arrived. These settlers were to get grants of 200 and 100 acres each. After twenty-one years the Colonial Office would then give the company a further 500,000 acres. To Stirling and Peel the plan looked very remunerative.

In 1829 Captain Charles Freemantle sailed into the Swan River and formally took possession of one million square miles of the new Western Australia. Shortly after this the first settlers sailed from England with ideas of rich living to be had in this new land. Unfortunately their ship, the *Parmelia,* ran aground and the new colonists found themselves sitting on the rocks surrounded by *'the emblems of civilisation they were to plant in the wild: cases of flour, trunks full of nankeen and velvet, Georgian furniture and rusting shovels'*.[8]

This was only the start of their problems, as they had to cope with barren soil, thickly wooded areas and constant mosquito bites. After the second ship bringing settlers was also wrecked on arrival, James Stirling as Lieutenant Governor had to work very hard to keep up the morale of his new colony. Thomas Peel was no financial manager and had omitted to tell the Colonial Office that one of his backers was a Jewish ex convict, Solomon Levey who had made good as a merchant banker and landowner. Peel had thought it best to keep this partnership a secret for fear of upsetting the colonists. As the money began to dwindle Levey contacted the Colonial Office to ask what was happening in the Swan River area but they were loath to tell him, as they had no record of his involvement with the project. Thomas Peel lived on in poverty and by 1832 the Swan River colony had just under 1,500 colonists most of whom would have returned to England if only they had the chance.

In 1839 after Stirling left, the Swan River colony was just about self-supporting but all the wheat and flour still had to be brought in from Hobart and the only export to England were a few hundred bales of wool each year. By 1850 after 20 years of settlement the population of Western Australia was only 5,886. Manpower was sadly lacking and all was *'depression, stagnation and, I may say, despair'*.[9] There was one way out, to use convicts.

No more convicts were sent to the east of Australia after 1852 but between 1850 and 1868, a total of 9,668 were sent out to the colony at Swan River, and by 1871 the population of Western Australia had increased to around 25,500.

The first view of Australia that James James would have seen was a low coastline broken by two rocky islands. As the ship drew closer he saw some wild heathery scrub and sparse trees but his first impression of the town of Freemantle may have reminded him a little of England. The houses were made of white stone and the pretty seafront was welcoming and cheerful.

In small groups the prisoners were disembarked and taken first to the bathhouse, and then into a large courtyard to be shaved and have their hair cut. The convict's hair had been cut fairly short in England but *'what they leave on there was a luxuriant growth compared to what they leave on in Australia'*.[13]

The prison building at Freemantle was a huge grey forbidding structure with thick grey glass windows keeping out the light, but in the strong sunshine of Australia this was sometimes welcome. Compared with the strict routine of an English prison with its doors and bars and officers at every corner, James James and the others were mainly left to carry out the discipline of the prison themselves. Officers here were on duty just to keep order and as long as there was no disturbance they did not interfere. Convicts also found their cells completely different from the iron cages at Portsmouth. They were whitewashed and stone built with an airy window, and best of all the doors were always left open except at night.

The Australian prison system was aimed at dealing with men who when released would form a very large part of the country's population. Consequently daily routine inside the Freemantle prison provided time for exercise and self-improvement. Convicts were put to the work that was most suitable for them and they enjoyed a plain but substantial diet. As long as the convict worked steadily the time passed and he soon became eligible for his ticket-of-leave.

In the height of an Australian summer the heat was very troublesome and some of the men who were sent to work outside the prison found conditions intolerable. Road-parties around Freemantle and Perth came under the close scrutiny of the public and therefore had to show prison vigilance and severity. With hot sand, biting insects, and little shade convict labourers suffered greatly.

Some of the luckier convicts were sent to work in the bush, and they felt that working away from the main establishment was *'better than anything inside the walls of a prison'*. The road-party would have to stay away from the prison for several days and during this time they lived in huts. The roofs were made of the rush of the blackboy (grass-tree) which kept the huts cool in summer and warm in winter and the beds inside were made of the same rushes which if kept clean would keep away insects during every part of the year. *'A hut is, in this country, one of the cleanest and most pleasant habitations you can have'*.[14]

It was during some of these expeditions into the bush that convicts often made attempts to escape. Although generally the prison system was sensibly managed, if a man tried to escape the punishment levied was truly terrible. The introduction of the 'chain gang' put these men in *'heavy irons in a separate dark cell for from fifty to a hundred days, with a diet of water and one pound of bread. The irons weighing, some of them, twenty-eight pounds were not to be removed day or night'*.[15]

Far from stopping escape attempts this punishment only made the men more determined to seek their freedom, and the heavier the irons were the more they tried to break free. On release, these men often became very hard and a danger to the community.

James James became eligible for his ticket-of-leave about the 5th March 1863 and received it two days later. Eligibility was based on the length of sentence, how long a man had been in prison in England or the colonies, and his behaviour. After 1857 a system of marks was also introduced which could be earned towards release.

The ticket-of-leave, or parole system, required a convict to report to the police at regular intervals, keep a steady job and avoid contact with other ex-convicts. Before release a convict had to decide what work he wished to carry out in the community and apply to potential masters for a job. Occasionally a ticket-of-leave was granted for a man to set up in business on his own but as he needed to convince the magistrate of his suitability for this option this was often refused. Convicts became increasingly despondent about having to stay in one area, and the laborious work of obtaining transfer documents which could take as long as a fortnight, deterred many of them from applying to another master in a different district. Sometimes the convicts failed to find a master to give them a job and in this case they were set to work at a government depot probably on road building much the same as the work carried out whilst in prison. *'Once sent on depot, there are many hundreds who, except for a month or two in the year, never leave it'*.[16]

Whilst James James was working on his ticket-of-leave he lost no time in applying for a conditional pardon. On receiving this conditional pardon James knew that he would basically be a free man. He would not be allowed to return to England before the term of his original sentence had expired but he would be able to travel within Australia and even overseas if he wanted too. If he returned to England and was caught he would have been convicted and transported a second time.

James should have received his conditional pardon on the 7th September 1863 but an unfortunate incident delayed matters. He was convicted of assault by the resident magistrate at Freemantle on the 13th July 1863 and was fined 5/- sterling. He finally received his freedom on the 22nd December 1863.

Moving south from Freemantle, James James found work wherever he could and eventually settled in Dardenup, a small area near Bunbury in the Wellington district. It was not difficult to find a plot of land to rent or buy for a nominal sum and once a small hut had been built to keep out the elements a man could begin to forget past misery. James would have called on his Forest of Dean skills to set up a small farm known as a 'station' with maybe a few goats and as in his youth he probably had a pig or two. The climate made it possible to grow a variety of vegetables and fruit and it was even possible to grow grapes for winemaking. Meat was available by hunting in the forests, kangaroo tasted like beef, opossum like rabbit and kangaroo rat like chicken. Then there were pigeons, parrots, emus and wild turkey and if the hut was near a lake there was always a plentiful supply of fish. By June 1868 James James was settled enough to employ his own ticket-of-leave man, convict no. 8643, George Pollard.[17]

In 1877 James married Selina Godden in Busselton, also in the Wellington district, and shortly after that the pair moved north to a small town called Toodyay on the Avon River. This area housed one of the convict depots and had a large population of convicts, ticket-of-leave men and expirees. It may be that James James went there to obtain workers, or just to find companionship after several years of working for himself. Whatever the reason, he obviously settled in Toodyay as first Catherine was born in 1878 followed two years later by Frederick.

Stanton Springs is a small area in the Avon Valley just downstream from

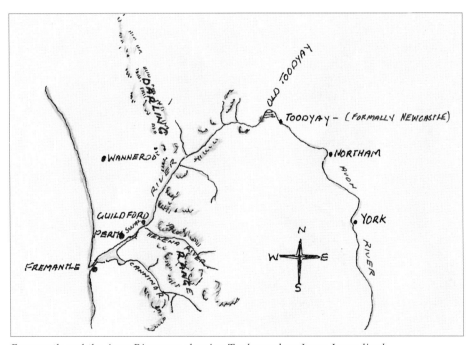

Freemantle and the Avon River area showing Toodyay where James James lived.

131

Toodyay. Here on the 11th October 1882 James James was found dead. He was 48 years old. His third child, a daughter, Margaret was just a few months old.

No prisoner in Western Australia ever really lost the label of 'convict' and these released prisoners were said to lower the tone of the colony. Eventually the British Government decided that transportation was becoming an expensive punishment and home imprisonment was costing less than had been expected. English prisons were not full, a new prison had just been built at Chatham and the hulks at Bermuda had been broken up. In 1865 a Prisons Act was passed which gave the Home Office the power to introduce more severe deterrent punishment for prisoners at home. It was felt that this new system could not be achieved by transportation, only by a hard regime of 'reformatory' confinement, followed by penal prison labour. This system continued until 1894 when it was seriously criticised, and successive governments began a slow change of attitude towards prisoners.

On the 12th October 1867 the last convict ship sailed for Western Australia, marking the end of an important aspect of Australian history and of the penal practice of the United Kingdom.[18]

Thomas STEPHENS

Thomas Stephens was the only one of the original men from the Forest of Dean who was not sent to Bermuda. Because of his illness he spent his first year of imprisonment at Dartmoor Prison. On the 21st October 1852 he was marched through the great stone archway bearing the inscription '*Parcere Subjectis*'[19] and escorted to his cell, where he was registered with the number 1577.

The Prison on the Moor had originally been built to house French prisoners of the Napoleonic wars. Although the main buildings of the prison were built by the winter of 1807 it was far from finished. The roofs were still to be slated and the officers' houses still had bare walls. It was decided that to put prisoners into such basic surroundings in the depth of winter would be cruel but it took so long to finish the building that another winter passed and it was not until May 1809 that the first draft of 2,500 prisoners were marched up from Plymouth. By the end of June, 5,000, the full number for whom accommodation had been provided, had arrived.

American prisoners from the War of Independence had been housed in two old line-of-battle ships at Plymouth but by 1813 enforced idleness and overcrowding was causing very serious discontent. The Admiralty became increasingly alarmed and in April 1813 250 American prisoners were removed to Dartmoor Prison. There followed a few years when 8,000 to 9,000 French and American convicts lived and worked side by side in great hardship and appalling conditions, but by 1816 the last prisoner of war had been returned home and the noise and bustle of Dartmoor was stilled, the gates were locked and the massive buildings left, no doubt to the countless numbers who had died there.

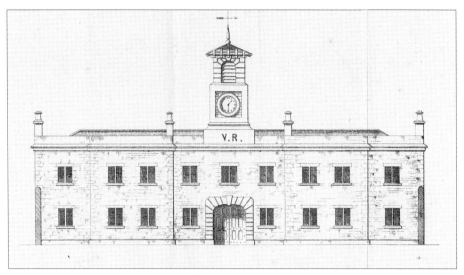

Elevation of Dartmoor Prison, 1851, taken from Report on the Discipline and Management of the Convict Prisons, 1850.   courtesy Glos. Records Office

Several schemes were considered for the future of the old war prison at Dartmoor and in 1818 Sir Thomas Tyrwhitt suggested that the formation of a railway from Dartmoor to Plymouth would enable the profitable export of granite, peat, iron, copper, and tin. Sir Thomas had dreamed for many years of flourishing farms on the moor but with the prison gone the village of Princetown also began to disappear and so he became desperate to revive the area together with his own prosperity. Although Tyrwhitt put many ideas forward he knew that the one idea that had ever made Dartmoor 'pay' was the housing of convicts. He was very pleased, therefore, when a Committee of the House of Commons held an inquiry into prisons and proposed the conversion of Dartmoor Prison into a prison for convicts adding, '*if it remains unoccupied, it must inevitably fall into decay*'. The report went on to say that '*Dartmoor abounds with granite of excellent quality, well adapted for the purpose of building or paving. Your Committee conceive that convicts would be capable of cutting granite to any extent for such purposes and that such a process would cleanse the land and fit it for cultivation*'.[20]

Tyrwhitt's plans all failed and for 20 years the old prison sat sadly on the moor with just basic maintenance work to keep the buildings in sufficient repair. In 1836 it was proposed to convert the prison into accommodation for 700 juveniles but the estimated cost was too great and the scheme was abandoned. In 1846 the 'British Patent Naphtha Company' took over the prison to produce chemical products from the peat but this proved almost unsaleable and after a few years the Company closed its doors.

By 1850 the removal of convicts to the colonies had virtually ceased with Western Australia the only place still receiving them. This situation meant a sudden demand for new prisons in Britain to accommodate the steady stream of prisoners pouring forth from the courts. Millbank and Pentonville were full to overflowing and prisoners were housed in the army barracks at Shorncliff and on the *Defence* hulk anchored at Portsmouth. It had been the practice for many years to ease the overcrowding in prisons by housing convicts on aged men-of-war specially hulked and refitted for the required task. Basically, all the equipment used for sailing the vessels was removed and a planked wooden roof was built over the upper deck to keep the weather out. This certainly extended the working life of these old frigates but conditions on board them were generally appalling. Prison hulks were also established at the Crown colonies of Gibraltar and Bermuda where new public works were being undertaken, but still the need for prisons grew. The Government was ready to take over any building that could be adapted to house prisoners and it was decided that the old war prison of Dartmoor would be ideal to house those 'invalid' convicts who were disqualified by age or infirmity from earning a living in the colonies. The situation of Dartmoor with its healthy climate and a wide area available for out-door employment seemed particularly suitable.

In November 1850 a small party of 70 convicts arrived from Millbank together with eight warders, Mr. Morrish the Deputy Governor and an escort of the Fourth Regiment. A few days later, Captain Gambier, the first Governor brought another 115 convicts and the work of converting the prison began. By the end of December considerable progress had been made in the repair of the different buildings necessary for accommodating 1,300 convicts. Two large buildings were to house 700 invalids *'who will sleep in large open dormitories, in hospital beds and hammocks. Two others are being fitted up with small sleeping-cells divided by corrugated iron partitions, on the plan of Portland, and will accommodate from 500 to 600 able bodied convicts'*.[21] One of the first prisoners to arrive at Dartmoor painted an inscription on an old piece of iron which read *'J. Wallace, 7 years - 1849 from Newcastle-on-Tyne, NO BACCY O DEAR, 1851, Hurra for Dartmoor and Cpt. Gambier.'*[22] To raise a 'hurra' for Dartmoor obviously meant that in spite of unpleasant living conditions and no tobacco the conditions at Dartmoor must have been far better than at Millbank. Certainly, Sir Joshua Jebb, the Surveyor General of Prisons hoped that by providing a good diet at Dartmoor he would encourage good conduct and hard work. The convicts were given white bread instead of brown in quantities more than the average man could eat and they were even allowed beer on Sundays. Hungry local children who lived on the moor would often visit the prison to fill their baskets with food rejected by the convicts.

However, these well-intended privileges had little or no effect on the convicts. Dartmoor was never built to hold men in cells and prison life was extremely hard for both convicts and warders owing to the conditions. The cells were permanently wet, drinking water was rationed and the frequent brutality of the warders meant that escape attempts were numerous and often successful.

In November 1852, one month after Thomas Stephens arrived at Dartmoor, a convict named Barrow disappeared from the gasworks. Stolen clothes were later found in Plymouth, but the man was never found. Stephens may well have been in the party of 100 convicts who in February 1853 went out in a blizzard to cut a track through the snow for the meat wagons to reach the prison. One man escaped but was recaptured the following day almost frozen to death.[23]

Fanny Stephens was finding it hard to make ends meet back home in the Forest of Dean. As a widow she was dependent on the parish for poor relief and she desperately missed the income which her son Thomas had provided from his work at the colliery. She was also convinced of her son's innocence, and with the help of some others, and after writing to Thomas, she raised a petition to the Secretary of State for the Home Department which was received on the 4th February 1853. In it she stated that she was unable to look after herself and this was supported by Henry Poole the incumbent of St. Paul's, Parkend, the assistant curate, one of Thomas's employers, the local schoolmaster and about 20 others.

At the same time, Thomas Stephens raised his own petition with the help of a solicitor in which he pleads *'that he had neither hand nor part in the commission of that offence, nor did he even know at that time, what had actually taken place'*.[24]

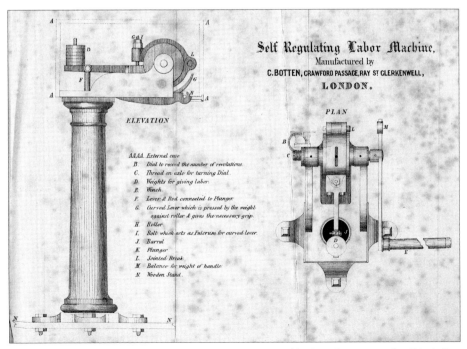

A Self Regulating Labor Machine at Dartmoor in 1850. Taken from Report on the Discipline and Management of the Convict Prisons, 1850. courtesy Glos. Records Office

To vindicate himself further he asked '*Was it possible for a female, surrounded by so many men, and labouring under great mental excitement, to recognise and positively swear to so many persons, when it appears the offence was committed before the dawn of day, and all the men were strangers to her?*' The petition ends '*Petitioner trusts, that in considering his case, his course thro' life, as regards character, which was never stained, but always consistent with that of an honest, hard working man, may not be lost sight of, and that sufficient pounds may exist to justify a mitigation of his long sentence. Your Petitioner as in duty bound, will ever pray, (signed) Thomas Stephens*'.[25] The plea for clemency was refused, and so his sentence of transportation for fifteen years remained.

Hard labour at Dartmoor obviously increased the fitness of Thomas Stephens. On the 2nd March 1853 he was put on board a ship for Gibraltar where he was to spend the next six years imprisoned on the Rock.

From the beginning of the eighteenth century Gibraltar had a small quay, and was the first overseas base for the Royal Navy. After the capture of Minorca, with its natural deep-water harbour at Mahon, Gibraltar took second place in the Mediterranean. In 1800 Malta gave the Navy a much-needed base in the

The entrance to Dartmoor Prison.   Averil Kear

136

eastern part of the Mediterranean and the base at Gibraltar was relegated to a supply depot and place for minor repairs. A resurgence of activity happened during the latter part of the Napoleonic wars when a large victualling station was built which was to be a great asset to fleets in the Mediterranean, providing them with much needed food and supplies.

In 1833 the dockyards at Malta were rebuilt to a much higher standard and the small repair yards at Gibraltar were again found to be unnecessary, and a new use had to be found for the moles. The base was just the right distance from British ports for passenger and cargo ships, on their way round the Cape to India and beyond and these ships started to use Gibraltar as a refuelling station. Spanish labour was used to carry coal and supplies to warships and merchant vessels. This was no easy task when the sea was choppy as the usual method was for the labourers to carry baskets on their heads. As the weather was so unreliable, it was decided that a breakwater would be useful and the British government designated convict labour for this operation. The first 200 convicts were sent out on the *Owen Glendower* in 1842. After the 'New' Mole[26] was completed, more parties of convicts were sent out from England to maintain and rebuild walls. There was plenty of work for them to do and even after the official ending of transportation prisoners were still being sent to Gibraltar. It took until 1875 for the British government to discover that by using local workmen they could save a great deal of money.

Thomas Stephens arrived on one of these working parties in 1853. Under the direction of the Royal Engineers he encountered a harsh regime in Gibraltar. Over one thousand men lived in a two-storey prison block on the waterfront. In the prison grounds were huge mantraps sprung open at night to catch any would be escapees. Every day working parties were marched out of the prison wearing their distinctive stiff broad arrowed uniform and red neckerchiefs. The men were manacled by the hundred as they were taken up the mountain to carve great pieces of the Rock. Yet others were taken to the naval dockyard, which was their normal place of work. They earned tuppence a day here, and if they had the misfortune to be given a job which involved working in the water they were allowed an extra drink of grog.

The sewers discharged their effluent directly into the harbour where the convicts were working and it was no wonder that many men suffered with virulent disease. In 1854 there was a Yellow Fever epidemic and many convicts who contracted the disease were housed aboard the *Owen Glendower*, which had now become the hospital ship. The Spanish authorities allowed a village to be constructed for the troops and civilians at the north of the island to try and keep them away from any contact with the prisoners. Dr. John Hennen who was the chief medical officer of health felt sure that the only way to stop these diseases was to burn the shacks and establish a new drainage system. But before anything could be done he himself died in the 1854 epidemic, which claimed the lives of 1,667 people.[27]

The convicts in Gibraltar were not effective workers, as they were given no incentive in the way of remissions for good conduct. They did enough work to keep out of trouble but were always on the lookout for a means of escape. This usually happened by stealing a boat and rowing across to the Spanish mainland where there was no extradition. Everyone on Gibraltar knew when an escape had taken place, the guns boomed and a white flag with five black crosses was flown from the Signal Station masthead.

On the 16th December 1857 Stephens was sent to England on board the *Lady McNaghten* for release on license.[28] He was the first of the men from the Forest of Dean to be released and his imprisonment had left him bitter in mind with a body that was pathetically thin after years of a diet of pea soup and gruel.

1 PRO HO 18/833
2 *Report on the Discipline and Management of the Convict Prisons, 1850* - Jebb p. 19
3 *A letter from a convict in Australia to his brother, 1866* (Cornhill Magazine 1866) p. 498
4 *Crime Law and Order in Mid-Victorian Portsmouth* - Edwards pp. 21-22
5 *Victorian Prison Lives* - Priestley p. 193
6 PRO HO 18/833
7 *Ibid.*
8 *The Fatal Shore* - Hughes p. 576
9 *Ibid.* p.577
10 *Ibid.* ref 3
11 *Ibid.* ref.3
12 *The Prison Ships* - Bateson p. 374
13 *Ibid.* ref.3
14 *Ibid.* ref.3
15 *Ibid.* ref. 3 p. 506
16 *Ibid.* ref 3 p. 508
17 Mrs. Beverley Iffla, Convict Historical Research Group, W. Australian Genealogical Society
18 *Convicts and the Colonies* - Shaw p. 358
19 'Parcere Subjectis' Spare the vanquished. (Remember, Roman, that it is for you to rule the nations, this shall be your task to impose the ways of peace, to SPARE THE VANQUISHED, and to tame the proud by war). Virgil - Aeneid 6. pp. 851 - 853
20 *Prison on the Moor* - Atholl p. 80
21 *Report on the Ddiscipline and Management of the Convict Prisons 1850* - Jebb
22 *Prison on the Moor* - Atholl p. 80
23 *Dartmoor Prison* - Rhodes p. 115
24 PRO H18/352/25
25 *Ibid.*
26 'Mole' A massive structure, especially of stone, serving as a pier or breakwater, or as a junction between two places separated from each other by water. Hence metonymically the water-area contained within the mole, an artificial harbour, a port. A New English Dictionary. Oxford University Press 1908
27 *Proud Fortress* - Andrews p. 148
28 PRO PCOM2/11

Chapter Twelve

BUT I AM HERE ALIVE TODAY

Richard Kear and George Charles turned the corner and started the walk up Viney Hill, which was the final part of their journey home. Their thoughts were very mixed. Would they be accepted back into a community which had disowned them some twelve years earlier? Would their friends and workmates speak to them and more importantly, what would be the feelings of their families after such a long absence?

They were excited as they walked up the hill with the sweet smelling ferns brushing their legs. They had forgotten how grand the oak trees were and memories of their childhood returned as they thought of the rough and tumble of climbing through the shady branches. There were a couple of small quarries on the hillside which neither men remembered, but the Albion Inn was just the same and they wondered if the cider was still as strong. They passed by St. Swithins School, which had only just opened when they left. It seemed larger and there were many more children playing in the yard. Richard thought of his own daughter Phoebe who was just a baby when he left. How would he ever get to know her now she was twelve years old?

Suddenly they were at Dead Man's Cross. The beech trees towered above the little track leading away to Danby Lodge and on still further to Blackpool Brook. Richard thought of the days spent fishing with his brother and sisters. He would soon know what had happened to his family whilst he had been away. He felt a slight sadness at the recollection that his father and mother had died whilst he was in prison and decided that he must visit their grave very soon. As he turned his head to the left he could see Oldcroft enclosure with the track leading up to his house and his heart raced.

Now there was an even sadder moment as the two men realised that after twelve years spent in each other's company they had reached the point where they would have to part. The others who had been arrested on that fateful occasion had all gone their different ways and two of them had found a final resting place in a setting far different from the wooded hillsides of the Forest of Dean.

George Charles and Richard Kear had been committed to the same prisons throughout the term of their confinement, but now they had to return to their own homes. The two men made quick arrangements to visit the families of

Thomas James and Hiram Archer to offer their condolences and to try and meet up with Henry Shapcott's family, They knew that whilst they were free men in that summer of 1863, Henry was still being held in prison. They knew too, that Thomas Stephens had been imprisoned in Dartmoor, as he was not well enough to be sent to Bermuda. They probably did not know that he was then sent on to Gibraltar and it is not certain if they ever saw him again

After a firm handshake George turned towards his house, which was just through Oldcroft enclosure and down the hill on the other side. Richard walked on up the road a short way and turned left through the clumps of foxgloves along the track by Cut and Fry Green. He stopped as his cottage came into view.

Richard Kear's cousin William had bought one of the three Kear homesteads at Oldcroft from his uncle in 1850 and when in 1854 William was bequeathed the adjacent plot by his father Thomas he turned both the houses into an inn known as the Loyal Forester.[1] The third plot, which had been left to Richard in his father's will, had been occasionally let out but had never been sold. The rent from the property had been paid to Phoebe as expressed in the will of her grandfather in 1858, until Richard returned to rightfully claim his property.

Richard wanted some time and space to readjust after he returned home and above all he wanted a degree of privacy after years of living cooped up with hundreds of other men. He was not best pleased to find that a window had been cut into the wall of an adjacent cottage, which directly overlooked his garden. One of the first tasks that Richard undertook was to ask his neighbour to block the window up.[2]

Bermuda Dick's house, Oldcroft. This was built by his father in 1830 and can be seen on plot 387 on the Encroachment map on page 8.

After Richard had gone, life had been hard for his mother. Mary had to care for her husband who was a cripple and for a while she had to share her home with Charlotte, Richard's wife, and baby Phoebe. Worn out with hard work, Mary died in 1859, just a year after her husband, and was buried next to him in the churchyard at Parkend.

With the help of her mother and father-in-law, Charlotte struggled for nearly four years to feed and clothe herself and her daughter. She had been told that her husband had been transported for life and to her that meant that he would not be returning. She was still a young woman and when she started to receive the attentions of Richard Powell, a collier from Coleford, she realised that life had to go on. She knew that she would be unable to survive without poor relief for very long and the opportunity to escape from inevitable degradation and despair led her to accept his offer of marriage just three years after her first husband had been transported. Like the rest of the Kear family Charlotte had kept very quiet about the events leading up to Richard's imprisonment and friends soon believed that Richard had died abroad. Charlotte Kear was noted as being a 'widow' when she married Richard Powell on the 4th November 1854 at the Registry Office at Westbury-on-Severn.

By 1863 Charlotte and Richard Powell were living in Ruspidge. They had three children, Elizabeth, Naomi and Richard, and Phoebe was also living with them. Divorce was not an option considered by the ordinary people in the Forest of Dean in the mid-nineteenth century and although Charlotte's marriage was bigamous she had no reason to believe that her first husband would ever return home again.

It is not known if Richard was aware of the sequence of events which had taken place whilst he was away, or indeed if he really cared, but he certainly wanted to know about his daughter Phoebe.

After a few days catching up with his sisters Jane, Eliza and Harriett, Richard Kear decided that the time had come to meet his daughter again. Phoebe had probably not been readily accepted into the new Powell family, especially when Richard and Charlotte started having their own children. Young Phoebe had remained close to her Kear grandparents and must have been saddened when they died within two years of each other. Although she was living with her mother and stepfather she often visited her grandparents at Oldcroft so it is not surprising that by 1867 she had returned to live with her father in the old homestead.

At the age of 16 Phoebe met Eli Green who was the same age and before long their relationship had produced a baby girl, Annie Maria. Phoebe and Eli went on to have another baby, Miriam Elizabeth in 1871 before they finally married at St. Johns Church, Cinderford on the 2nd December 1872. Phoebe and Eli set up home together and went on to have several more children who loved to visit their grandfather at his cottage at Oldcroft.

Richard and George had a much more difficult task when they visited the parents of Thomas James and Hiram Archer. They were able to tell the families of the trials and tribulations of the Bermuda imprisonment and the time spent in Millbank and Portland prisons before leaving England. Hiram Archer's widowed mother introduced the two men to her grandson and was proud to tell them that he had been named Hiram after his uncle.

George Charles had been luckier than Richard when he returned to Oldcroft as both his parents, Mary and Thomas were still alive. George resumed work as a collier but many long years of imprisonment had taken their toll on his health. He never married and died at the age of 47 in 1875 shortly after his close friend Richard married for the second time. In George's will he left his parent's house to his nephew William and another smaller property to his niece Eliza Beach.

Henry Shapcott was to outlive both George and Richard, not dying until 1906. He married Elizabeth Cinderey at Holy Trinity church, Drybrook just a year after his release, and the couple settled down in Newnham where Henry ran a successful coal merchants business in the High Street. Business was good and their comfortable lifestyle even allowed them to hire Sarah James as a domestic servant. They produced two children, Elizabeth and William, and after Henry died, his will proved in Gloucester on the 29th June 1906 left everything to his widow.

Until Phoebe married and moved out of the cottage at Oldcroft, Richard had to look after her and her two daughters for a few years and it became important for him to gain employment. Like many other coal miners in the Forest of Dean he went where the work was offered.

The Forest of Dean in the mid-nineteenth century was still in a most lawless state with many men unemployed and fighting just to survive. It is no surprise that the first murder of a Gloucestershire police constable took place in August 1861 near the Speech House shortly before Richard returned home.

By 1871 there were nearly 3,000 miners[3] working in both large and small pits dotted throughout the Forest. Miners were experiencing great hardship and many men had to resort to sheep stealing and other theft just to keep their families fed. Illicit drink was brewed and consumed in large quantities so that the colliers could have at least some escape from the long hours underground with only very meagre pay for their efforts. A few strong willed colliers prompted their colleagues to strike for better working conditions and in September 1871 the first miners' trade union was formed. On the 13th February 1872 a particularly large group of colliers led by Goode, Ferris and Tyndall marched behind a band fervently playing 'Stand like the brave' towards Crab Tree Hill and Trafalgar Collieries. The police turned out in force to prevent any disturbance and after an interview with Edwin Crawshay, who was one of the Forest magistrates, the men returned to their homes. The next day at the Turpin Mine Pit a more serious disturbance took place led by a collier named Beach and the two Kilbey brothers. These three ringleaders were arrested and police were kept on duty all night to prevent any escape attempt.[4]

In the spring of 1874 the Sully brothers who owned the pits at Parkend attempted to cut the miners' pay by 25%. Timothy Mountjoy who was the miners' agent succeeded in reducing this to 10% but by November of the same year the Sully brothers were asking for a further 10% reduction in pay. The Forest colliers came out on strike and although the deepest snow for many years lay on the ground the conflict between the miners and their masters continued until the following January.

The miners were determined to succeed, despite the attempted intervention of Timothy Mountjoy who could see the inevitable outcome of the situation. The men wrote threatening letters to their employers accompanied by effigies of men in coffins. Policemen were issued with cutlasses as a protection and were stationed at each of the collieries. The enginemen consented to remain at work to prevent the collieries becoming flooded and as a precaution against this event all the horses were brought to the surface, which was a most unusual occurrence. Ultimately the miners were compelled to give way and work resumed. A great depression fell on the colliers after this conflict bringing poverty and starvation to many families. This was a time when many people emigrated to America, in particular Pennsylvania where the coal mining industry was crying out for workers. As he joined his comrades in their fight for justice, Richard Kear must have thought about his brother George who had emigrated all those years ago to the same place.

At the beginning of 1881 Richard, now aged 52, was working at Lightmoor Colliery. He was living at Oldcroft at this time and the trip to Lightmoor each

Lightmoor Colliery.   Ian Pope collection

day was quite a distance through the woods. Lightmoor was situated on the eastern side of the Forest of Dean about 2 miles from Cinderford. Very good quality house coal was produced here, at the rate of eight hundred tons a day, and was sent to markets as far away as Cornwall and Ireland. On the 27th May 1881 Richard was injured at the colliery by a roof fall. The injuries he sustained were obviously quite serious as he was taken to Gloucester Infirmary to have his wounds dressed.[5]

After Richard Kear returned to Oldcroft, he soon became part of the community again. He joined his mates after a days work for a jar or two in the Nag's Head but he never had too much to drink again as his increasing Methodist beliefs dictated that drink was an evil influence. Kear families had always been connected with the promotion of Methodist teachings in the areas around Parkend, Lydney and Yorkley and several chapels in the 1860s had members of the family on their church roll.

One of the early preachers in the Forest was Edward Kear, generally called 'Clergy Ned'. His reputation of giving powerful sermons was born out when he was preaching at Whitecroft once. He had no sooner read his text, *'for the great day of His wrath is come; and who shall be able to stand?'* than a man in the congregation called out, *'I shall'*. The preacher's rejoinder, *'Then you'll have to alter first'*, did not send the man home on better terms with himself or the preacher.[6]

Richard and his friends had held meetings for some time in temporary accommodation at Oldcroft and so he must have been pleased to hear in 1875 that a piece of 'open waste land' had been purchased to build a chapel for the 'Prims' at Oldcroft.[7] However, before the new building was erected another major event took place in Richard Kear's life.

In his younger days Richard had been very friendly with the Elsom family who ran the Jovial Forester alehouse at Yorkley. On his return to the Forest he met up again with John Elsom, now aged 52, who lived at Yorkley and still worked as a quarryman. Richard asked after the rest of the family and was told that all the girls including Mary had married. Richard was told that Mary had married a stonemason named William Morgan in 1857. The couple married in Gloucester but soon after their marriage William and Mary returned to the Forest to live at Pillowell. They had at least one child, a daughter named Sarah who at the age of 18 was working as a servant to Henry Clayfield, a grocer and draper living at Nibley in Blakeney. Sarah eventually married Mr. Knight and moved to Gloucester but remained very close to the Kear side of her family for the rest of her life.

Richard met up with Mary many times and after her husband died the relationship blossomed. They were married in St. Aldate's church in Gloucester on the 3rd April 1875. Richard was noted as being a widower on his marriage certificate even though there had been no formal divorce between him and his first wife Charlotte. Richard brought Mary and her children back to live in his house at Oldcroft and on the 18th December 1875 their only child, Richard was born.

The opening of Oldcroft chapel in 1876 meant that the congregation of 19 now had their own place of worship. The chapel, built at a cost of £306 became part of the Pillowell Circuit, which already included chapels at Viney Hill and Blakeney.[8] Richard Kear became a staunch member of the new chapel and by 1892 the Methodist movement was flourishing with Oldcroft chapel increasing its membership to 32. Richard junior was brought up to attend chapel probably twice a day on a Sunday and as he grew older he became a preacher on the Pillowell Circuit.

Richard saw great changes in the Forest of Dean during the latter part of his life. The Severn & Wye Railway opened for passengers on Easter Monday 1876. Richard, Mary and their baby may well have taken one of the train excursions to the Speech House on that day to enjoy pony rides, donkey, dog and man racing, and greasy pole climbing.

Railways and tramroads were extended from new pits to join up with the Great Western Railway and on the 17th of October 1879 the Severn Railway Bridge was opened amidst flag waving and cannon fire. There were river excursions to see the bridge, and on the hillside were swing boats, merry-go-rounds, and shooting galleries. The bridge was completed within 4 years at a cost of £200,000 and was to speed up the movement of coal from the Forest of Dean to all parts of the country.

When Richard Kear could not work anymore he tended his garden at the homestead at Oldcroft, growing enough vegetables to feed his family with enough left over to give to any neighbours. A few more cottages were erected in the village bringing the population to around 400, and a new church, All Saints was built in 1867 at Viney Hill.

> Richard Kear lived long enough to see his son marry Martha James at Viney Hill Church on the 24th March 1900. The young couple set up their home with Richard and Mary in the cottage at Oldcroft. Martha was the daughter of Joseph James whose younger brother Thomas died in Bermuda after contracting Yellow Fever.

On the 21st January 1901 young Richard and Martha had a son to be called Ivor Richard. Richard senior was introduced to his latest grandchild just two months before he died.

The Gloucester Journal listed the death of Richard Kear on the 9th March 1901 and he was buried in Viney Hill churchyard on the 13th.

Richard Kear junior became a pillar of the community, preaching regularly on the Pillowell Circuit and becoming a trustee of Blakeney, Moseley Green and Oldcroft chapels.[9] He became the secretary of the Sunday School committee and even after Oldcroft chapel was forced to close in 1929 after a storm had caused severe damage Richard continued his preaching at Viney Hill chapel. Richard junior also became a member of the Ancient Order of Foresters, which he joined in 1897. The group met regularly at Blakeney and in 1927 Richard was still a member having been responsible for raising considerable sums of money to help many needy miners and their families.[10]

His father would have been very proud of the report in the *Dean Forest Guardian* in March 1914 concerning the Yorkley chapel anniversary, at which '*Mr. Richard Kear of Oldcroft was the preacher*'.

'*Mr. Kear is known in the Forest as a clear, earnest and intelligent local preacher in the Primitive Methodist denomination to which, however, he does not limit his services as a preacher. On the contrary he is appreciated as such in other denominations as well as his own and his work on Sunday was no exception both as regards its own merits and the appreciation it won*'.

[1] Photocopy of a deed of William Kear's property dated 1893 in the possession of Mrs. A. Kear
[2] Story passed down through the Kear family.
[3] *Blood on Coal* - Anstis p.9
[4] *Journal of Police Superintendent Chipp* (In the possession of Mrs. Rosemary Howells) pp. 19-20
[5] *Dean Forest Mercury* 27.5.1881
[6] *The Methodist Recorder* Winter 1895
[7] Photocopy of conveyance of Oldcroft Chapel dated 1944
[8] GRO D2598 4/9 Pillowell Circuit Records.
[9] GRO D2598 4/6 Pillowell Circuit Records
[10] GRO D1125/4/1 Ancient Order of Foresters

Richard Kear (son of Bermuda Dick) and his wife Martha in later years. courtesy Norman Kear

Appendix 1: Personal and Prison Histories

HIRAM ARCHER

Born/Baptised	1826 Yorkley (Forest of Dean)
Occupations	1851 Collier
Addresses	1851 Yorkley
Married	Unmarried
Died	14.10.1853 Bermuda after contracting Yellow fever.
Children	No children

Prison Record

Littledean Prison	18.9.1851	Prison No. 5055
Petty Sessions	22.9.1851	
Gloucester Prison	22.9.1851	Prison No. 1668
Assize Court	2.4.1852	Transportation for life
Millbank Prison (London)	7.9.1852	Prison No. 23889
Edward Convict ship	22.11.1852	
Left England	23.1.1853 (on *Edward*)	
Arrived Bermuda	28.2.1853	
Medway Convict Hulk	28.2.1853	Prison No. 2056
Tenedos Hospital ship	October 1853	

GEORGE CHARLES

Born/Baptised	1829 Oldcroft (Forest of Dean)	
Occupations	1851 Farm labourer	1875 Labourer
Addresses	1851 Oldcroft	1875 Oldcroft
Married	Unmarried	
Died	1875 Oldcroft	
Children	No children	

Prison Record

Littledean Prison	4.8.1851	Prison No. 5034
Petty Sessions	5.8.1851	
Gloucester Prison	5.8.1851	Prison No. 1573
Assize Court	14.8.1851	Transportation for life
Millbank Prison (London)	17.12.1851	Prison No. 22544
Portland Prison (Dorset)	25.8.1852	Prison No. 2855
Edward Convict Ship	29.12.1852	
Left England	23.1.1853 (on *Edward*)	
Arrived Bermuda	28.2.1853	
Medway Convict Hulk	30.6.1853 - April 1861	Prison No. 2048
Left Bermuda	10.4.1861 (on *Sir George Seymour*)	
Arrived Falmouth (Cornwall)	11.6.1861	
Arrived Millbank (London)	12.6.1861	
Arrived Deal (Kent)	18.6.1861	
Arrived Gravesend (Kent)	18.6.1861	
Chatham Prison (Kent)	June 1861 - August 1863	

JAMES JAMES

Born / Baptised	1832 Yorkley (Forest of Dean)	
Occupations	1851 Collier	1881 Farmer
Addresses	1851 Yorkley	1881 Australia
Married	Selina Godden 1877 Busselton, Australia	
Died	11.10.1882 Stanton Springs, Australia	
Children	Catherine (born 1878),	
	Frederick (born 1880),	
	Margaret (born 1882)	

Prison Record

Littledean Prison	2.8.1851	Prison No.5034
Petty Sessions	5.8.1851	
Gloucester Prison	5.8.1851	Prison No. 1572
Assize Court	14.8.1851	Transportation for life
Millbank Prison (London)	17.12.1851	Prison No. 22543
Portland Prison (Dorset)	25.8.1852	Prison No. 2854
Edward Convict ship	29.12.1852	
Left England	23.1.1853 (on *Edward*)	
Arrived Bermuda	28.2.1853	
Medway Convict Hulk	30.6.1853 - Feb 1861	Prison No. 2047
Boaz Island (Bermuda)	13.2.1861	Prison No. 1810
Portsmouth Prison (Hampshire)	5.4.1862	
Left England	29.9.1862 (on *York*)	
Arrived Freemantle (Australia)	31.12.1862	
Ticket-of-leave granted	7.3.1863	
Conditional pardon granted	22.12.1863	
Fined for assault (Freemantle)	13.7.1863	
Released	August 1863	

THOMAS JAMES

Born / Baptised	1831 Neds Top, Oldcroft (Forest of Dean)
Occupations	1851 Collier
Addresses	1851 Neds Top, Oldcroft
Married	Unmarried
Died	7.10.1853 in Bermuda after contracting Yellow fever.
Children	No children

Prison Record

Littledean Prison	—	
Petty Sessions	—	
Gloucester Prison	9.8.1851	Prison No. 1596
Assize Court	14.8.1851	Transportation for 15 years
Millbank Prison (London)	17.12.1851	Prison No. 22537
Portland Prison (Dorset)	25.8.1852	Prison No. 2849
Edward Convict ship	29.12.1852	
Left England	23.1.1853 (on *Edward*)	
Arrived Bermuda	28.2.1853	
Medway Convict Hulk	30.6.1853	Prison No. 2045
Tenedos Hospital ship	October 1853	

RICHARD KEAR

Born/Baptised	1826 Oldcroft (Forest of Dean)	
Occupations	1851 Collier	1881 Collier
Addresses	1851 Oldcroft	1881 Oldcroft
Married	1) Charlotte Young 1850,	
	2) Mary Hathaway Morgan 1875	
Died	9.3.1901 Oldcroft	
Children	Phoebe Ann 1851,	
	Richard 1875	

Prison Record

Littledean Prison	1.8.1851	Prison No. 5032
Petty Sessions	5.8.1851	
Gloucester Prison	5.8.1851	Prison No. 1571
Assize Court	14.8.1851	Transportation for life
Millbank Prison (London)	17.12.1851	Prison No. 22542
Portland Prison (Dorset)	25.8.1852	Prison No.2853
Edward Convict ship	29.12.1852	
Left England	23.1.1853 (on *Edward*)	
Arrived Bermuda	28.2.1853	
Medway Convict Hulk	30.6.1853 - April 1861	Prison No. 2046
Left Bermuda	10.4.1861 (on *Sir George Seymour*)	
Arrived Falmouth (Cornwall)	11.6.1861	
Arrived Millbank (London)	12.6.1861	
Arrived Deal (Kent)	18.6.1861	
Arrived Gravesend (Kent)	18.6.1861	
Chatham Prison (Kent)	June 1861 - August 1863	
Released	August 1863	

HENRY SHAPCOTT

Born/Baptised	1832 Bristol	
Occupations	1851 Collier and Ag. Labourer	1881 Coal Merchant
Addresses	1851 Moseley Green and Etloe	
Married	Elizabeth Cinderey 1865	
Died	1906 Newnham	
Children	Elizabeth Cinderey 1866	
	William Henry 1868	

Prison Record

Littledean Prison	17.9.1851	Prison No. 5053
Petty Sessions	18.9.1851	
Gloucester Prison	19.9.1851	Prison No. 1661
Assize Court	2.4.1852	Transportation for life
1st Petition	13.4.1852	
Reply to Petition	22.4.1852	
Report on Case	5.7.1852	
Millbank Prison (London)	7.9.1852	Prison No. 23888
Edward Convict ship	22.11.1852	
Left England	23.1.1853 (on *Edward*)	
Arrived Bermuda	28.2.1853	Prison No. 2055
Medway Convict Hulk	30.9.1853 - 30.6.1859	Prison No. 2470

2nd Petition	6.5.1859
Boaz Island (Bermuda)	23.1.1862
Portsmouth Prison (Hampshire)	5.4.1862
3rd Petition	23.5.1862
Recommended for release	March 1863 & March 1864
4th Petition	2.4.1864
Released	August 1864

THOMAS STEPHENS

Born/Baptised	1830, Yorkley (Forest of Dean)
Occupations	1851 Collier
Addresses	1851 Yorkley
Married	Not known
Died	Not known
Children	Not known

Prison Record

Littledean Prison	1.8.1851	Prison No. 5033
Petty Sessions	5.8.1851	
Gloucester Prison	5.8.1851	Prison No. 1574
Assize Court	14.8.1851	Transportation for 15 years
Millbank Prison (London)	10.5.1852	Prison No. 23313
Dartmoor Prison (Devon)	22.10.1852	Prison No. 1577
Gibraltar	2.3.1853	Prison No. 2171
Left Gibraltar	16.12.1857 (on *Lady McNaghten*)	
Arrived England for release	December 1857	

Extract from OS 6inch Islands of Bermuda, 1901.
Crown Copyright Reserved

Appendix 2: Dates of Chief Admiralty Buildings

BERMUDA, THE GROWTH OF A NAVAL BASE
By paymaster Lieutenant W. E. Brockman
Royal Navy
(Member of the Society for Nautical Research)

Dates of Chief Admiralty Buildings 1795 - 1932

(Year given is that of commencement, where known)
The Royal Gazette and Colonist Daily, Wednesday May 25th 1938

1795 to 1809	Cottages on Hen Island, at St. George's
1809	Adaption of wharf for careening at St. George's.
	House and Tanks at St. George's.
1809	Guard House in Ireland Island.
1814	The Spar Yard.
	Blacksmiths' Shop (Spar Yard Theatre).
	A cottage ('Trott's Cottage').
	R.N. Hospital in Ireland Island.
	Cook and ratings' quarters at Royal Naval Hospital.
1815	Three houses overlooking Gray's Bridge, now two.
1816	Officers' house on North slope of Ireland Cove.
	House for the Commissioner (all demolished by 1827).
1818	Artisans' Houses near Portland Place (The 'Square').
1819	Junior Surgeon's House at Royal Naval Hospital (now Warrant Wardmaster's).
	Foremen's houses in Dockyard.
1821	Wine cellars and improvements at Admiralty House.
1823	Tank in the yard.
	Tank at Royal Naval Hospital.
	Clearing and blasting commences with convicts.
1825	The Commissioners House.
1827	The Cottage, The Parsonage, Fortifications and the Keep.
1838	Foundations of Lighthouse at Wreck Hill.
1840	Houses round Spar Yard. Boat Slip in North yard.
1841	Workmen's houses on Hospital Island.
1842	Main Gate and walls of North yard.
	Dockyard Guard house (Fleet Mail Store).
1843	South-West Guard house.
1844	Boys School.
1845	Plumbers Shop in Spar Yard.
	Albert Row (Four houses).
1846	Mortuary at Royal Naval Hospital.
	Gate Porter's Lodge at Royal Naval Hospital.
	Victoria Row (Eight houses).
1847	Four more houses at Albert Row.
1847	Boat repairing shed in North Yard.
	Stables and cart shed in Yard.
	The breakwater (North yard).
1849	The Victualling Yard.

to	Officers' house in dockyard.
1855	Terrace.
1850	Magazine on Sober Island (later Magazine Island and now 'elbow' of South breakwater).
	Bowe's Island Barracks.
1851	Shipwrights' shop.
	The Oratory (converted slave quarters at the parsonage).
	The Cooperage in North yard.
1852	Engineers' Smithery.
	Stone coal stores.
	Tide guage house (later diving store).
1853	Isolation quarters on Ports Island.
	Foundry and fitting shops in North yard.
1855	More officers' houses in Dockyard Terrace.
1857 to 1859	Naval Store Department Storehouse.
1858	More houses at Victoria and Albert Rows.
	Engine and Boiler house in North Yard.
1859	Boat shed in Spar yard.
	Engine House in Spar Yard.
1860	The Sail Loft.
	A further twelve houses at Victoria and Albert Rows.
	Tank under the Sail Loft.
	Gun mounting store.
1861	Wings of Royal Naval Hospital.
1862	The Flushing Engine.
1862	More quarters at Royal Naval Hospital.
	More tanks in the yard.
	Mast house and timber store.
1862 to 1867	Seven houses at Prince Alfred Terrace.
1868	The Saw Mills.
1872	Spar Yard Theatre (conversion of Blacksmiths' Shop).
	Officers' Billiards Room.
1875	Constructors' Repair Shop in yard.
1876	Engine house for sheers. (demolished in 1929).
	Officers' quarters at Ports' Island.
	Pitch house on North breakwater (now 'heads').
1878	Dispenser's House at Royal Naval Hospital.
	Cottages near Spar Yard.
	Captain-in-Charge's Bowling Alley.
	Post Office and semi-detached cottages to its west.
1879	Princess Louise Terrace (four houses).
1880	The Royal Naval Canteen.
	Cottages on Hospital Island.
	Captain-in-Charge's boat shed in Spar Yard.
1881	The Girls School.
	Shed on boat slip in North Yard.
	Railway lines in Yard.
1882	Galvanizing Shop.
	Royal Naval Officers' Club.

	Royal Naval Warrant Officers' Club.
1883	Plumbers' Shop and boiler house in yard.
1886	Single men's quarters at Maria Hill.
1887	Cable tanks.
1888	Torpedo boat slip in Spar Yard.
1889	Workmen's dining room.
1890	Additional quarters at Maria Hill.
1891	Boilermakers' shop.
	Torpedo workshop.
1892	Inspector of Shipwrights' house.
	Carpenters' shop in Spar Yard.
	More coal sheds.
	New Cut Bridge.
1893	Houses near Masonic Hall.
	Royal Naval Canteen Bowling Alley converted into Petty Officers 'Club'.
	Torpedo Store in Yard.
1899	More coal sheds (for 4,300 tons).
	The Zymotic Hospital.
	A house (now dental surgeon's residence).
1900	Moresby House (residence of Officer in Charge of Works).
1901 to 1905	Extension of Dockyard, South yard.
1930	Royal Naval Club cottages for staff.
	Extension of Royal Naval Canteen.
1932	Dockyard Recreation Club House.
	Extension of S/W, W/T Station at Royal Naval Barracks.
	Bowling Alley at Royal Naval Club.

The victualling yard, Royal Dockyard, Bermuda.   Averil Kear

Appendix 3: Memorable Events
during the life of Richard Kear 1826-1901

1824 First convict hulk arrives in Bermuda from Britain.

1826 Bell's harvester invented.

1829 Stephenson's 'Rocket', built.

1831 Dean Forest Riots. Warren James transported to Australia.

1833 Abolition of slavery in British Empire.

1834 Dorset 'Tolpuddle Martys' transported to Australia.

1836 South Australia becomes a British Province.

1837 June. Victoria becomes Queen.

1837 Charles Dickens, 'Oliver Twist'.

1839 Establishment of the Police Force in Gloucestershire.

1841 Steam driven forge hammer patented by Bourdon & Nasmyth, UK.

1843 Rebecca riots in Wales

1845 Irish potato famine.

1845 I. K. Brunel's 'Great Britain', first iron steamship to cross the Atlantic.

1847 Factory Act in Britain - 10 hour day.

1848 Public Health Act, Britain

1851 September. Opening of the South Wales Railway.

1859 Darwin, 'Origin of Species'.

1860 First underground railway in the world - London.

1861 Death of Prince Albert, Prince Consort.

1861 May. Bermuda's first Royal visitor. H.R.H. Prince Albert, pays a six day visit.

1862 The last convict hulk is decommissioned at the dockyard in Bermuda.

1867 All Saints Church, Viney Hill consecrated

1868 T.U.C. formed

1868 Opening of Yorkley Baptist Chapel.

1871 Stanley finds Livingstone

1874 Disraeli becomes Prime Minister.

1875 Telephone patented by Bell, UK & USA

1876 Opening of Oldcroft 'Bethesda' Chapel.

1878 Salvation Army created.

1879 Opening of the Severn Railway Bridge.

1879 Zulu war.

1892 First British Labour M.P. in Scotland. (James) Keir Hardie.

1894 Rudyard Kipling, 'Jungle Book'.

1900 First agricultural tractor in England.

1901 January. Death of Queen Victoria.

Bibliography

ANDREWS, Allen. *Proud Fortress: The fighting story of Gibraltar*. Evans Brothers Ltd. 1958.

ANSTIS, Ralph. *Warren James and the Dean Forest Riots*. Alan Sutton Publishing Ltd. 1986.

ANSTIS, Ralph. *Blood on Coal*. Black Dwarf Publications, 1999.

ANSTIS, Ralph. *The Story of Parkend*. Lightmoor Press, 1998.

ATHOLL, Justin. *Prison on the Moor*. John Long Ltd. 1953.

AYLING, Stanley. *John Wesley*. Collins, 1979.

BATESON, Charles. *The Convict Ships 1787-1868*. Brown, Son & Ferguson Ltd. 1985.

BENDER, John. *Imagining the Penitentiary*. University of Chicago Press, 1987.

BETTEY, J. H. *The Island and Royal Manor of Portland*. University of Bristol, 1970.

BRANCH-JOHNSON, W. *The English Prison Hulks*. Christopher Johnson. London, 1957.

BRIGHT, Thomas. *The Rise of Nonconformity in the Forest of Dean*. Privately published, Forest of Dean Local History Society, 1953.

CAMPBELL, Charles. *The Intolerable Hulks. British Shipboard Confinement 1776-1857*. Heritage Books Inc. 1994.

COLLEDGE, James J. *Ships of the Royal Navy: An Historical Index*. David and Charles, 1969

COAD, Jonathan. *The Royal Dockyards 1690-1850: Architecture and engineering works of the sailing navy*. Scolar Press.

COOKE, Arthur O. *The Forest of Dean*. Constable & Co. Ltd. London, 1913.

CURSON, H. *A compendium of the laws and government of England, Scotland and Ireland*. Printed London, 1699.

DAVITT, Michael. *Leaves from a prison diary Vol II*. London, Chapman and Hall, 1885.

DENT, Digby Henry. *Two Commissions*. Marshall Bros. London, 1899.

DOWNIE, Murdo. *Directions for making the Bermudas 1803*. B.J.A.M.H. Vol.9, 1997.

DUCANE, Sir George Edmund. *Account of the manner in which Sentences of Penal Servitude are carried out in England*. London. 1882.

EDWARDS, F. H. E. *Crime Law and Order in Mid-Victorian Portsmouth*. Portsmouth Papers No. 55, Portsmouth City Council. 1989.

ERICKSON, Rica & O'MARA, Gillian. *Convicts in Western Australia 1850-1887 Vol IX*. University of Western Australia Press.

EVANS, Lieutenant John. *Description of the coasts of Bermuda*. B.J.A.M.H. Vol 9, 1997.

FINDLAY, Alexander. *Description of the Bermudas or Somers Islands with Nautical Direction*. B.J.A.M.H. Vol 9, 1997.

GIBSON, Charles. *Life among Convicts, Vol II*. Hurst and Blackett, 1863.

GODER, Theodore L. M.D. *The Forty Thieves*. Bermuda Historical Quarterly Vol XIX No. 3. 1962.

GRIFFITHS, Arthur. *Memorials of Millbank and Chapters in Prison History, Vol II*. Henry S. King & Co; London 1875.

HARRIS, Edward Cecil. *Bermuda Forts*. Bermuda Maritime Museum Press, 1997.

HART, Dr. Cyril. *Free Miners*. British Publishing Co. Ltd. Gloucester, 1953.

HART, Dr. Cyril. *The Forest of Dean: A New History*. Alan Sutton Publishing Ltd; 1995.

HARVEY, Christopher, Surgeon Royal Navy. *Epidemics of Yellow Fever at Bermuda, 1853*. Bermuda Archives, 81/1772 and 89/3389.

HAWKINGS, David T. *Bound for Australia*. Phillimore & Co. Ltd. 1987.

HAWKINGS, David T. *Criminal Ancestors*. Phillimore & Co. Ltd.

HILLS, George. *Rock of Contention: A history of Gibraltar*. London: Robert Hale, 1974.

HOBSBAWN, E. J. & RUDE, George. *Captain Swing*. Lawrence and Wishart, 1969.

HOLLIS-HALLETT, Clara. *Bermuda's Convict Hulks*. B.J.A.M.H. Vol. 2, 1990.

HUGHES, Ann (Editor). *17th century England – a changing culture 1618-1689*. Ward Lock Educational and the Open University, 1984.

HUGHES, Robert. *The Fatal Shore*. Pan Books, 1987.

IGNATIEFF, Michael. *A Just Measure of Pain*. Pantheon Books, New York, 1978.

JACKSON, Sir William G. F. *The Rock of the Gibraltarians*. Gibraltar Books Ltd. 1990.

JEBB, C. B. Lieut-Col. *Report on the Discipline and Management of the Convict Prisons, 1850*. H.M.S.O. London, 1851.

JEBB, C. B. Lieut-Col. *The Penitentiary in the Industrial Revolution 1750-1850*. Pantheon Books, New York. 1978.

KERHALLET, Philippe de. *Considerations Generales sur L'Ocean Atlantique*. (4th edition 1860) B.J.A.M.H. Vol 9, 1997.

KISSACK, Keith. *Monmouth: The making of a County Town*. Phillimore, 1975.

LAWRENCE. Revd. George E. *Three Strands of Methodism in the Forest of Dean*. Lecture to Wesley Historical Society, 1977.

LAWRENCE. Revd. George E. *Kindling the Flame: 150 years of Methodism in the Forest of Dean 1824-1974*. Published by the Author, 1974.

LOVETT, William. *The Life and Struggles of William Lovett*. Published by the Author, 1876.

MACDOUGALL, Philip. *Royal Dockyards*. David and Charles, 1982.

MALDWYN-HUGHES, H. *Wesley and Whitefield*. National Council of Evangelical Free Churches, London, 1912.

MAYHEW, Henry & BINNY, John. *The Criminal Prisons of London*. Frank Cass & Co. Ltd. 2nd Edition, 1968.

MITCHELL, E. *The Bermuda Convict Establishment, 1863*. B.J.M.A.H. Vol. 9, 1997.

MOUNTJOY, Timothy. *The Life of a Forest of Dean Collier*. Privately published, 1887.

NICHOLLS, H. G. *Forest of Dean*. David and Charles, 1966.

OWEN, Barbara. *James Kear J.P.* Privately published, 1989.

POTTER, Dennis. *The Changing Forest*. Secker and Warburg, 1962.

PRIESTLEY, Philip. *Victorian Prison Lives*. Pimlico, 1999.

QUINN, David. *Bermuda in the age of exploration and early settlement*. B.J.A.M.H. Vol.1, 1989.

REID, Colonel (Sir W.), Governor of Bermuda. *On the Winds and Navigation of the Bermudas, 21.3.1846*. B.J.A.M.H. Vol.9, 1997.

RHODES, A. J. *Dartmoor Prison*. Bodley Head Ltd; London.

RUDE, George. *Criminal and Victim*. Clarendon Press, Oxford 1985.

RYLE, J. C. *Select sermons of George Whitefield*. Edinburgh: Banner of Truth Trust, 1958.

SHAW, A. G. L. *Convicts and the Colonies*. Faber & Faber, 1966.

SPUFFORD, Margaret. *Small Books and Pleasant Histories*. Methuen, London, 1981.

STONE, Lawrence. *Road to Divorce. England 1530-1987*. Oxford University Press, 1990.

STRATFORD, Joseph. *Good and Great men of Gloucestershire*. C. H. Savory, Cirencester, 1867.

STRANACK, Ian. *The Andrew and the Onions*. The Bermuda Maritime Museum Association, 1990.

SWEENEY, Christopher. *Transported in Place of Death*. Macmillan Co. of Australia Ltd. 1981.

SYDES, William alias JONES. *Account of life on the convict hulks, 1838-1845 by one of the prisoners*. Bermuda Historical Quarterly Vol. VIII Winter, 1951.

THOMSON, Basil. *The Story of Dartmoor Prison*. Heinemann, 1907.

TROLLOPE, Anthony. *The West Indies and the Spanish Main*. Alan Sutton Publishing Ltd. 1985.

TROTTER, A. W. *The Dean Road*. John Bellows, Gloucester, 1936.

TYERMAN, Rev. Luke. *The Life of Rev. George Whitefield*. Hodder and Stoughton, London, 1876.

VEREY, David. *Diary of a Cotswold Parson*. Alan Sutton, 1978.

WATERS, Brian. *The Forest of Dean*. J. M. Dent & Sons Ltd. London, 1951.

WHITING, J. R. S. *A House of Correction (Littledean)*. Alan Sutton Publishing Ltd. 1979.

WHITING, J. R. S. *Prison Reform in Gloucestershire*. Phillimore, 1975.

WILKINSON, Henry C. *Bermuda from Sail to Steam*. Oxford University Press, 1973.

WILLOCK, Roger. *Bulwark of Empire*. Bermuda Maritime Museum Press, 1988.

WOOD, James. *The Laws of the Dean Forest*. H. Sweet, London, 1878.

WOODWARD, E. L. *The Oxford History of England: The age of reform 1815-1870*. Clarendon Press.